Praise for *DEI: How to Succeed*

CW01065097

This book is like the experienced senior D
Working in DEI can feel like a lonely place
and only DEI professional in your organizat.... Sarah takes you through
a journey: by starting with a very practical and hands-on perspective on
how to set up your DEI strategy for success to checking in with yourself
and defining your values and personal boundaries in the job. Most
organizations aspire for diverse and inclusive workplaces that foster a
sense of belonging we as humans need to thrive. This book shows the
actual steps to make it happen.

*Floria Susan Moghimi, Consultant, Speaker and Managing Director at Floria
Moghimi D&I*

***

Akin to the title itself, Sarah in this book has achieved a near-impossible
job of creating a practical toolkit for every DEI professional and leader
today. DEI, contrary to perception is not the cherry on the cake of
company culture; it is the cake itself, and in this book, Sarah
accomplishes to write up the recipe.

Manjuri Sinha, Global Director of Talent Acquisition at OLX Group

***

Sarah's *DEI: How to Succeed at an Impossible Job*, is **THE** book that every
DEI practitioner around the world needs to keep on their desk! No
matter where you are in your DEI journey this book gives you first-hand
insight on how to create an effective DEI strategy that includes
extremely useful tips but it also includes an "instead try this" section that
is even more helpful to read! From the beginning of the book, Sarah sets
the stage by asking the reader to imagine that she is having coffee with
them and sharing her expertise with a peer. This book will help you make
informed decisions, but more importantly, it will make you feel like you
are not alone in this important journey!!

*Camille Kelly, Chief Diversity Officer of Future Talent Council and CEO &
Founder of CKC Solutions LLC*

I love that Sarah goes further than needing executive buy-in to make DEI progress by providing "the how" to weave DEI into the business. Without this approach, DEI lacks sustainment to make real change.

Ellen Bailey, *Speaker, Moderator and VP of Diversity and Culture at Harvard Business Publishing*

***

The thoughtful approach and practical guidance of this book are incredibly valuable for both new and experienced DEI practitioners. As more and more companies are starting their journey towards creating a more diverse, equitable, and inclusive workplace, this book is an excellent resource and essential reading for anyone driving this change within the organization. It will help set them up to successfully deliver on what sometimes seems like an impossible task.

Jessica Gedamu, *VP Global Diversity, Equity and Inclusion at Springer Nature*

***

This book is the manual every DEI practitioner needs as their guide throughout their journey in this sector, which is incredibly challenging, complex and most of the time with limited resources to hand. Sarah's holistic approach to this important role gives readers the tools and insights to navigate the many twists and turns we face in this profession which at most times can feel quite daunting. A great and must-read!

Vanessa Sanyauke, *CEO & Founder, Girls Talk London*

***

Would you like to feel as if you are having a coffee talk with one of the most competent DEI experts in Europe? Then grab this book. In 7 chapters, Sarah tangibly guides you through the challenging yet rewarding reality of corporate DEI — a must-read for anyone starting their career in DEI.

Samet Akti, *Sr. D&I Communications Manager at Zalando and Keynote Speaker*

Sarah skillfully uses her vast experience in the diversity, equity, and inclusion (DEI) field to help newbies to the topic kick-start the work. I wish I had this book when I was starting my D&I journey.

Sandra Subel, *Global Head of D&I at Axel Springer*

***

This book is a rewarding read. It is indeed a guide professionals in this space have been waiting for. It summarises yet breaks down the common problems faced in this role with much clarity. One can consider it a handbook for both newcomers and seasoned professionals. It brings in practical guidance yet encourages further research into organizational context and history because no two companies are the same.

Yvonne Obi, *Organisational Psychologist and Diversity & Inclusion Global Manager, Booking.com*

***

In plain language, Sarah lays out the realities and challenges of being responsible for starting the DEI journey of a company. If you are new to the work or struggling with progress, this book will help you and your leaders get started (or restarted) in the right way.

Nichelle Appleby, *Director, Reward and People Digitalization at wefox*

***

I loved every bit of this book, for so many reasons. First, this book is very relatable. Sarah shares with us real-life experiences she's gained from her career, which makes this book very easy to understand. Secondly, Sarah does not stay at a theoretical level but suggests many practical situations and solutions to commonly-faced challenges. They are very actionable, 'do-it-next-day' solutions. Finally, the one thing I really loved about this book is though it's applicable for any location, it's written in the context of Europe which we have not yet seen many publications focusing on. If you don't know how to start D&I in your organization, this is your book.

Mertcan Uzun, *Head of Culture & Community at Blinkist*

DIVERSITY, EQUITY & INCLUSION

How to Succeed at an

Impossible Job

SARAH CORDIVANO

Diversity, Equity and Inclusion: How to Succeed at an Impossible Job.
First Edition. Copyright © 2022 by Sarah Cordivano
Imprint: Impossible Press

The opinions expressed by the Author are not necessarily those held by their employer or sources referenced in this book.

Ordering Information: quantity sales and special discounts are available for quantity purchases by corporations, associations and others. For details contact: BookInquiries@SarahCordivano.com

Cover design by Giorgi Nanava, gnanava@gmail.com
Illustrations by @buddi2019 on Fiverr

ISBN:

979-8-9866578-0-6	Paperback
979-8-9866578-1-3	Hardcover
979-8-9866578-2-0	eBook

Library of Congress Control Number: 2022914009

The information contained within this book is strictly for informational purposes. The material may include information, products or services by third parties. As such, the Author does not assume responsibility or liability for any third-party material or opinions. Readers are advised to do their own due diligence when it comes to making decisions.

10 9 8 7 6 5 4 3 2 1

ACKNOWLEDGEMENTS

This book would not have been possible without:

- My friends working in DEI. Conversations with you over coffee, a drink or zoom have been the inspiration for this book.

- The generous and insightful feedback readers: Tanja Slišković, Floria Moghimi and Jessica Gedamu. Tanja, thank you for encouraging me to think more academically while writing this book. Floria, thank you especially for your suggestion to add in the *How to Hire a DEI Consultant* section. Jessica, thank you for encouraging me to include some of the things I've learned from challenges we faced in our work. Thank you *all* for your thoughtful comments and advice.

- My partner Elad who is skilled at both close reading and offering his perspective at a distance.

- Friends and family who have offered their support and encouragement along the way.

- My teammates (current and former) working side-by-side to create change, often against great obstacles.

- Designer, Giorgi Nanava, who designed the cover of this book and a lot more. Thank you for bringing your creativity, ideas and willingness to experiment in order to communicate this book in the best way possible.

- Everyone in my life whose ambition, vulnerability and courage has inspired me to turn this idea into reality.

- And *everyone* working hard in their spare time to create change in the world we live in, through activism, volunteering and community work. Your hard work is a true inspiration.

Lastly, a huge acknowledgment and appreciation for the vast network of supportive and collaborative people in DEI around the globe, working tirelessly to make small changes that have big impact.

TABLE OF CONTENTS

PREFACE

This book is a concise introduction to getting started with Diversity, Equity and Inclusion (DEI) in the workplace. It provides practical step-by-step guidance to common challenges in organizational DEI, including setting a strategy, putting in place governance through a DEI council, estimating budgets, measuring results and communicating with your audience. It explores DEI initiatives to create a more inclusive working environment. This book is most useful for individuals tasked with the immense challenge of starting their organization's DEI efforts from scratch and who need some help figuring out where to begin. This book is written to be specifically relevant for European-based organizations as well as ones with a global footprint.

This book will help you understand:

- ❏ Who are the main stakeholders that are critical to the success of your work

- ❏ How to create a DEI strategy that has buy-in among our stakeholders and is impactful and achievable

- ❏ How to measure your success and communicate your progress

- ❏ How to launch impactful DEI programming that addresses the needs of your organization

- ❏ How to build an inclusive organization with programs that support leaders and employees to understand their role in inclusion in the workplace

- ❏ How to think about your relationship with your DEI role and how to protect yourself from emotional burnout

I hope this book can help you along your journey and offer some direction to a vast and complex undertaking.

MEET THE AUTHOR

Hi. I'm Sarah. I wrote this book you are about to read. I've been working in DEI in Berlin in different roles and for different companies. I've worked as a DEI team of one and as part of a team of ten. I've also worked 1:1 with emerging tech companies to help them think about DEI before growing to become future unicorns. Throughout this, I've been co-organizing a discussion group with others working in DEI in Germany. When I noticed some of the conversations keep repeating, again and again, I realized I wanted to write this book. The challenges we all face are similar; the methods for dealing with those challenges also have a lot in common. This book was born from these casual conversations often over coffee, and so I tried to keep that same tone in this book. When you read it, imagine we are having a coffee together, sharing ideas and commiserating over failures. This is not a rigid how-to guide, but rather a reflection of what I've learned while working in DEI and an invitation for discussion, in the hope you find it useful for discovering your own path.

I'll tell you below a little more about myself, growing up near Philadelphia in the US, studying geography and public policy and then focussing my career on data analytics, project management, community building, then ultimately DEI. I can already tell you that the biggest lesson from my professional journey is that having a background in as many fields and places as possible offers a sharpened toolset for a career in DEI. Simply: a "linear career path" is overrated. Here's how I got to do what I do and learn what I've learned to navigate into a successful DEI career. Your story will be very different, but perhaps this will encourage you to recognize the "other" parts of your journey which may not be obviously related to your final destination. Those are precisely the parts that will give you special powers and much-needed perspective in your day-to-day.

To start at the beginning: my dad is a mushroom farmer and my mom is a librarian and educator. I was always fascinated by maps and travel. I studied geography, urban studies and data analytics. This gave me a taste of how resources and opportunities are inequitably distributed and introduced me to the tools to measure that inequity, diagnose the problem and propose solutions. I researched and published on the topic of access to maternity care and came to understand that what *should* be a human right is often lacking, especially along racial and class lines. The most important technical skill I developed was how to use data to answer complex questions.

I worked in city government as tech support for government employees who used mapping software in their department's operations. This taught me to explain technical and non-technical concepts in a simple and clear way. I also learned that I loved working with people and connecting them with resources, answers and other people doing similar work.

I also worked as a project manager at a software company. I became experienced at organizing big client projects with a lot of moving pieces (alternative job title: Cat-Herder-in-Chief?). But this also exposed me to something more life-changing: the tech industry, in all its promises and all its flaws. I saw first-hand how tech companies can have good intentions but under the guise of AI-fueled "smart" solutions can create harmful and damaging technology that poses an immense risk to our society. I can't unsee how "world-changing tech" often directly contributes to inequality through data bias and poorly thought-out decision making. Through this work, I also got into community building and founded a meetup for digital mapmakers in Philadelphia.

In 2016, I moved to Berlin as a sort of reboot of my life. As I got acquainted with the Berlin tech scene, I became aware of Employee Resource Groups. I found that the skills I picked up over the years — community engagement, project management and data analysis — are incredibly useful in the context of DEI, which in Europe was just emerging as a relevant topic in the workplace. I transitioned into working in DEI full-time, bringing along the skills I built throughout my career. Project management allowed me to approach DEI in an organized and operational way. Community building and public policy allowed me to understand stakeholder motivations and put sound governance in place. And data analysis allowed me to define metrics, measure outcomes and tell apart the interventions that sound good on paper, from the interventions that actually work. The base skills you bring to your DEI work will be different than mine — the trick is to make them work for you in the context of this evolving profession.

Here are a few things I learned along the way, which also happen to be the themes that will show up again and again in this book:

1. Accepting my career path as having a non-linear trajectory helped me navigate challenges and take hold of opportunities that forced me outside my comfort zone and find out what I truly enjoy working on.

2. Bringing together skills I've learned through various professional, educational and social aspects of my life immensely helped me think about DEI not as a purely academic or professional pursuit, but as something much more nuanced and complex. This allowed me to approach the field of DEI in a realistic, pragmatic way.

3. Data is the sharpest tool in our toolbox. It enables us to truly understand the problems we are trying to solve *and* tell a compelling story. It helped me move away from anecdotes and assumptions and think about the *actual* problem we are trying to solve.

4. Self-care, emotional distance and resilience have been incredibly important to me for a sustainable job in DEI. But even with that said, I am not sure if I personally feel that DEI can really be a *forever* career for most. I believe DEI practitioners should strive to excel and make a difference; but they simultaneously should make sure they're strengthening the transferrable skills, the ones which will be useful throughout any career shift they might pursue.

And finally, a message to you from me: I want this book to be a comforting hug to every person working in DEI who is struggling, as a team of one, maybe even doubting their decision to take this path. I want this book to be a reminder that we need to be humble, realistic and pragmatic in the work we do and grant ourselves the permission to manage our own expectations and the expectations of others. This book is for every single person who finds themselves somewhere along the *working student* -to- *DEI manager* -to- *burnout* pipeline, trying their best. I hope it challenges us all to think beyond the passion that compels us and discover the keys to success to achieve the impossible. Let's do this together… by focusing our attention on the fundamental building blocks of success and creating a healthy relationship with the work itself.

WELCOME

When I started my first DEI job several years ago, I needed a book like this. I had a solid understanding of DEI concepts and understood how to manage big, strategic projects, but bringing those two things together was not at all easy. I also struggled with meeting the expectations of all my stakeholders which were much higher than what I could manage as the only DEI role in a big company. Over the years, I have had many, many conversations with friends and colleagues facing similar problems. These conversations helped me find solutions and deal with the emotional weight of this unique role. And they also helped me think more deeply about the work we do, why we do it and how we can do it better. Sometimes these discussions revolved around solving a specific challenge, like implementing an inclusion and identity survey. At other times, these conversations helped me put words and structure to the feelings of frustration I've faced trying to advance DEI in a corporate setting. No matter the topic, I've always had moments of revelation in these discussions. The most important revelation is: the biggest, stickiest challenges I've faced are also being faced by many other people working in DEI. With that in mind, I started writing a blog[1] to share the outcomes of those 1:1 discussions with everyone else facing the same challenges. Ultimately, those discussions inspired this book: a practical, holistic guidebook that shares the step-by-step solutions for starting DEI work from scratch.

Many of these problem-solving discussions have been with others in Europe who have found themselves in DEI roles not because it was their chosen career path but because they've been appointed to do so. Whether they were in an HR generalist role, a corporate strategy role or a passionate member of an Employee Resource Group, they found themselves inheriting ownership for this work and struggling to begin. In fact, the in-jest working title of this book was "So You've Been Voluntold to Lead DEI, Now What?" No matter how you found yourself here, I hope this book can make the journey a little less chaotic and terrifying.

This book is uniquely targeted towards anyone staring down the seemingly impossible task of building a DEI strategy from scratch to carry their organization into the modern age. This book will be especially useful for the lone DEI practitioner who does not have the luxury of being supported by a team of specialists and experts. I've presented the chapters in a roughly chronological order to offer a logical series of steps to get started. Each thematic part includes practical approaches to the everyday challenges of DEI in the workplace. The language is intended to be welcoming and easy-to-digest, without the density of an academic text. I tried to write this book as if *you and I* are having a conversation over coffee. Because to be honest, a lot of the ideas in this book came together over exactly such casual discussions. You can read it through as

---

[1]Some of the sections of this book originally appeared in some form as blog posts at *https://medium.com/sarah-cordivano*. The versions included here have been adapted for this book.

an entire book or in pieces as challenges come your way. There is no right or wrong way to read this book, use it however it is most helpful to you. I've also included reflection questions in the appendix to help you think about how each chapter is relevant to your work and how you can put the guidance into practice.

But let me also manage expectations (an essential skill in a DEI role, by the way). This book can't and won't solve every challenge. I've focused on the universal challenges that myself and others have come across in guiding an organization toward competency in DEI, but of course, not everything will be covered. I've purposely targeted this book to the challenges of a European based company or an organization with a global footprint with different needs across its locations. This book is probably most helpful if you are based in Europe because much of the insights draw from my experiences working with European companies.

It's also important to tell you upfront: I don't spend any time in this book *convincing* you that DEI is important and necessary in your organization. This book assumes some core knowledge around DEI and an understanding that this work is vital. If you are not yet in that mindset, take some time to read about the value of DEI and the societal and systemic issues that lead to inequality, exclusion and discrimination.[2] Part of the journey to becoming personally bought in to the value of DEI is embarking on that learning journey in your own way and discovering what is compelling and meaningful to you. If you do not personally see and feel the value of DEI, it's challenging to convince others of that.

So, with all that said, let's dive in.

---

[2] With contributions from many DEI practitioners, I've compiled a list of books and podcasts on DEI and social justice: *http://resources.sarahcordivano.com/*. You can also find a *Further Reading* section in the appendix with a list of books relevant to the topic of each chapter of the book.

PART 1:
INTRODUCING ORGANIZATIONAL DEI

Diversity, Equity and Inclusion take different forms in different spaces. The size of your organization, its structure, the cultural and geographical context, history and much more will influence what will be the most impactful approach for you. Because of this, it's important to have a wide perspective on what DEI is and how it may fit into your work. So, let's take a moment to define some terms and concepts used in this book.

What are organizations and who are the key players?

Before we talk about diversity, equity and inclusion in the workplace, let's talk about *the organization* where people work. When I refer to *organizational DEI*, I'm talking about how organizations think about and implement DEI in the workplace. An *organization* in this context typically means for-profit businesses or companies, but it could also mean institutions such as universities. In general, most of the advice in this book is particularly relevant for medium to large organizations (500-20,000 employees). This is not because this approach is somehow unique to them, but because those organizations are most likely resourced enough to thoughtfully consider DEI but not too large that they've started their journey years before. But no matter the size of your organization, you may still find this book helpful. The advice in this book is particularly beneficial for organizations with a European or global footprint, who need a DEI approach that is globally relevant. Therefore, I've purposefully avoided focusing this book on one geography, such as the US or the UK.

Much of the guidance of this book assumes your organization has a leadership structure with a team of executives (sometimes referred to as the executive or management team). This is the team that makes top-down strategic decisions, is responsible for executing those decisions and allocates resources such as staff and budget. Typically, organizations also have a broader team of senior managers (sometimes defined as Director level and above) that is referred to as a Senior Management Team or Senior Leadership Team. This book also assumes some sort of hierarchical structure in an organization, meaning reporting lines that eventually report to the executive team.

A critical partner in the success of your DEI work is the Human Resources (or HR) team. This team typically drives recruiting, hiring, performance management, learning and development, compensation and other employee-centric topics. HR's involvement is crucial to implementing a successful DEI strategy, but they are far from the *only* partner that should be involved.

In communicating your messages and programs, the Communications Team becomes very important. The Legal Team is key to understand what local legal regulations and guidelines are necessary to follow. Another essential stakeholder group is Employee Resource Groups (or ERGs). ERGs are employee identity or experience-based groups that build community. ERGs are generally focused on building and providing support to their community, collaborating with the organization on decisions that affect their community and raising concerns on behalf of their community. If your organization has an ERG[1] program, these groups will be an integral part of a successful DEI approach.

You likely have additional stakeholders who will be involved in your DEI work in one way or another. DEI is a topic that benefits greatly from spending the extra time to seek out all the relevant stakeholders and fully understanding their involvement in your work and their own motivations.

What is Diversity, Equity and Inclusion?

Now that we've defined the landscape in scope for this book, what does DEI actually mean?

Diversity encompasses all the ways in which people are different. That includes visible and non-visible differences like race, ethnicity, gender, age, cultural background, socio-economic background, religion, sexual orientation, disability, languages spoken or life experiences. These differences shape who we are as human beings; they influence our thinking and perspective. What does this practically mean? Where we grew up and what languages we speak will impact our options and choices for education. The cultural norms around us will influence how we communicate about ourselves and about others. And many other aspects of our identity will determine what opportunities and resources are available to us.

Inclusion means creating an environment where people feel comfortable being themselves and bringing their differences with them, where they feel valued and welcome, especially if they're different from the majority. Inclusion is necessary, especially for a diverse workforce,

---

[1]Part 4 of this book: *Everything About Employee Resource Groups* is focused entirely on this topic, so don't miss that if you are interested in setting up an ERG program.

because it ensures everyone is heard and able to contribute no matter who they are. When an organization is actually inclusive, employees should be able to show up as their authentic selves without hiding parts of their identity for fear of exclusion.

Equity refers to working towards fair treatment, access, and opportunity for all people. Equity can be promoted by identifying and eliminating systemic or individual barriers that prevent full participation and engagement of all groups and individuals. Organizations improve equity and increase fairness by recognizing and addressing institutional and environmental systems of injustice and oppression as well as unequal distribution of opportunity.

Getting Started with DEI in the Workplace

What does this all mean in the workplace? These concepts touch on almost every part of the employee experience. Where to begin? I see many organizations that are eager to focus on diversity initiatives first. They want to enact initiatives that focus on hiring from diverse groups of people, as fast as possible. This is a shortsighted approach. Efforts to diversify your workforce do not exist in a vacuum.[2] Well-intentioned hiring initiatives will fail if there are discriminatory or exclusionary structures in place undermining your efforts. I'm referring to issues like unfair compensation, promotions without transparency, biased hiring and discriminatory behavior. What typically happens is newly hired employees join but quickly realize the workplace is not welcoming, fair or supportive and then they leave. This type of diversity-hiring revolving door does a lot of damage to workplace culture and can cause harm to

---

[2]"On its own, demographic diversity is not enough to drive change within an organization. Employees must feel included as part of their local teams and as valued, respected members of the larger organization. Building an inclusive culture is a shared responsibility of employees, managers and organizational leaders; it takes intention at every level to sustain an inclusive workplace." Gallup, 2018. *Three Requirements of a Diverse and Inclusive Culture — and Why They Matter for Your Organization.*
https://www.gallup.com/workplace/242108/diversity-inclusion-perspective-paper.aspx

employees. We'll explore this in Part 5: *Launching a holistic diversity hiring program.*

So how does inclusion and equity fit together with diversity? Diversity initiatives cannot be successful without first listening to your existing employees and addressing the challenges they face relating to inclusion and equity. This requires reviewing internal processes across the board (hiring, performance evaluation, promotions, compensation, company culture, ethics, benefits including health care and family leave, speak-up systems) with an eye for inclusion, fairness and anti-discrimination, to figure out where your problems truly lie. This step requires a joint effort with leaders, HR and process owners across the organization who must be willing to critically review these processes and make changes.

At the beginning of the journey, this organizational self-reflection will help you understand what barriers exist and where you should focus your effort. But it also needs continuous attention as you move ahead with your initiatives because some of these barriers and challenges only become apparent as DEI work intensifies. You will repeatedly find new inclusion and equity challenges through conversations with employees or through seeing the difficulties firsthand while implementing your work.

DEI initiatives generally exist somewhere along a spectrum from non-controversial community-building work to very difficult organizational change. It's relatively easy for everyone to get on board with the community-building activities (such as movie nights organized by the ERGs). But it takes a lot more dedication, courage and effort for everyone to get on board for the *real* work. I'm referring to the challenging work that forces an organization to face their issues head-on and grapple with the unfairness, discrimination and bias built into their processes.

I've found DEI work to be less like compliance topics which demand adherence to strict rules and regulations. It, instead, requires reviewing and changing processes and getting decision-makers bought in and committed to the idea that DEI should be considered in their strategic decisions. That work requires resources (time and budget) and, more importantly, the will of the organization to strategically prioritize DEI work and change processes. This is where transformational work *truly* lies.

What is the difference between internal and external DEI?

There are two main types of DEI work: internal and external. In order to set realistic goals and expectations, you need a strong understanding of the scope and critical stakeholders for both types. Most of this book deals with internal DEI, but there is sometimes a gray area where these two spheres overlap.

Internal DEI refers to everything relevant to the employees, internal processes and organizational culture. Internal DEI work will focus on inclusion and equity among employees. This typically includes hiring and equitable promotions, improving internal processes, conducting inclusion surveys and supporting Employee Resource Groups. In this scope, the relevant stakeholders are typically HR, hiring managers, leadership teams, the legal team, and the compliance team. Depending on your organization, there may be other essential stakeholders.

External DEI refers to everything relevant to *external stakeholders* including customers, suppliers and partners. External DEI work typically focuses on the diversity of suppliers, inclusion of customers and supporting an external ecosystem that is equitable and inclusive.

To make this a bit more concrete, let's use an example of a tech company that builds a social media platform. An external DEI strategy will likely focus on creating an accessible platform and ensuring that it is inclusive for all potential users, including advertisers and partners. It could also focus on the content shared on the platform to make sure it meets a code of conduct. Finally, it may include policies for the broader social media ecosystem by partnering with external organizations to facilitate industry-wide change.

Though the main focus of this book is on the internal side of DEI, there are situations where these two spheres of DEI overlap, so it's good to be aware of the distinction. In my view, it's crucial to have a diverse, equitable and inclusive workplace before trying to tackle challenges on the external side. But it is possible to focus on the internal and external sides simultaneously if you have strong stakeholder buy-in and there are sufficient resources (meaning staff and budget) to accomplish the work.

Why is DEI an impossible job?

In many ways, a DEI job is an *impossible* job. I don't mean that it's impossible to do really great work and create impactful change in the work you do. I mean it's often impossible to achieve *all* the things you want in your DEI work. Simply put: the expectations of the role often do not live up to the reality of what can and will be accomplished with the resources and commitment you have available. When companies hire their first Head of DEI, they tend to pass on years' worth of back emails (concerns, complaints, ideas) and expect them to be immediately addressed with new initiatives and programs. Similarly, companies sometimes expect that a lone DEI role can single handedly change their organization without being offered the budget, resources and internal willingness to actually create change. The extent of what can be achieved by the DEI team is limited by what the organization is *willing* to do. This conflict of intentions, expectations and possibility is rarely transparent to everyone involved. Once you understand the situation you are working in and these limitations, you can figure out how to move beyond them.

This misalignment of expectations as well as under-resourcing creates a lot of frustration for everyone involved. I've found one of the main reasons for this is that by the time an organization decides to hire someone in a DEI role, there's a lot of frustration already building within the organization. This could be frustration following an internal incident of unequal pay, a very public sexual harassment case or a general frustration at the lack of diversity in leadership. When the DEI role is eventually created, there's finally an outlet for employees' frustrations, ideas and expectations. But of course, it then becomes a very tall order to meet all those expectations quickly, especially when you are just getting started in the role. But why are the expectations from DEI roles so high, and how can you do your best to manage them?

Acknowledge the emotional weight of the work

First, let's acknowledge the elephant in the room: DEI is not like other jobs. In most jobs, when your day is over, you can clear your mind of your work responsibilities and think about something else. Unfortunately, I've never found that to be the case with DEI work. Why is that? DEI is a hugely emotional topic. Every element of diversity is a deeply personal topic for *someone* in your organization. In many cases, you are dealing with topics that are also deeply personal to you and carry significant emotional weight. Being in charge of DEI typically means you (understandably) are the person employees reach out to when the organization fails them. Typically, by the time you get an email from an employee, the organization has already failed them in a significant way. When employees don't feel a sense of inclusion, their wellbeing suffers.[3] Your role here becomes part therapist, part problem-solver.

One of the specific challenges is mentally processing these complaints and then figuring out what is actionable in the context of the DEI strategy you want to achieve. These conversations hopefully give you some insight about what's going on in your organization. This is helpful in shaping your strategy. But employees also want to see change

---

[3]"The effort it takes – physical and emotional – to deal with micro-incivilities can lead to burnout, depression and reduced performance. Race–related stress is one of the greatest sources of stress at work, according to Wing Sue. In other words, dealing with micro-incivilities matters if you are at all interested in having high–performing teams." Pearn Kandola, 2018. *How micro-incivilities can impact wellbeing.*
https://pearnkandola.com/diversity-and-inclusion-hub/bias/racism-at-work-micro-incivilities

happen quickly. It can be tempting to put in new DEI programming based on individual concerns. Unfortunately, this tends not to be a sustainable approach to addressing DEI holistically. This challenge underscores the importance of having a strategy in place early on to guide your work. A strategy helps you avoid reactionary problem-solving, which will spread your efforts too thin to be impactful. We'll talk later about how to build a meaningful strategy that addresses the core challenges of your organization and puts you on a long-term path towards success (see: Part 3: *How to create your organization's first DEI strategy*).

There's another reason why DEI jobs tend to be "impossible." Passionate people hoping to enter the DEI field often assume that these jobs are a utopia of fulfilling and rewarding activism work.[4] After beginning their DEI jobs, one of two things typically happens. They become quickly disillusioned, feeling that they have to compromise their values in a corporate world. Or they become the torchbearers of activism, and quickly crash and burn against a backdrop hostile to in-house activists. To me, productive DEI work feels quite different from activism in its traditional sense. In my experience, successful DEI work centers on slowly advocating for organizational change through building strong stakeholder relationships. Change happens gradually, through advocacy and through awareness of what *can* be achieved within your organization. Sustainable change requires aligning the interests of many, many people with vastly different motivations. This specific realization can be a tough one, because it continuously forces DEI professionals to see our work in a different light than how our families, friends, colleagues, and even ourselves, think of it.

---

[4]To read more about the realities of DEI jobs: *How can I get a job in DEI (Part 1)?* Aubrey Blanche, 2019. *https://blog.usejournal.com/how-can-i-get-a-d-i-job-bcc0b32a3c81*

Move from the *impossible* to the *possible*

How to turn an impossible, frustrating, burnout-prone job into a rewarding job that you can succeed at? The most important thing is to have clarity about your role and be able to communicate expectations to your stakeholders. Here are some tips for success:

1. Get clarity on whether your role focuses on internal or external DEI or both. If your organization has just begun its journey, I'd suggest beginning by focusing on internal DEI. Once you know what your scope will be, set boundaries and be transparent about what *isn't* your responsibility.

2. If you are working on DEI in addition to another role, get clarity on how much time you should spend on DEI work and how to manage or reduce other work responsibilities. Never accept the task if you are not explicitly allocated time for it.

3. Prioritize putting a DEI strategy in place as your first order. A DEI strategy helps you focus your efforts and protects you from interruptions and temptations to work on new initiatives or expand your scope. Make sure the strategy is fully communicated and signed off by the leadership team.

4. Hone your understanding of *what is* and *what is not* in your power to change. Then, focus your time and efforts on what *can* be changed. At the same time, try to assess whether your organization is ready and willing to whole-heartedly address DEI. If they are not willing to critically examine their processes, tackle the difficult challenges or offer you the resources you need, they may not be taking DEI seriously, and it may not be worth your time and effort.

Even with all these tips, DEI is still an extremely difficult job. It comes loaded with so many expectations. These expectations come from ourselves about what we want to personally achieve, they come from our colleagues about what kind of change they expect to see in the workplace and they come from leaders regarding how much they are willing to give up[5] to see change. It will always be impossible to meet everyone's needs. So, the one piece of advice I'll add here is: try to take some of the pressure off yourself to meet *everyone's* expectations. Try to find the levers where your effort and time is most well spent and focus on that. In Part 7: *The Job & You*, I revisit this topic of *DEI as a job* and try to put all of this into the broader context of what we are trying to achieve and how we can do that without burning out.

---

[5]This doesn't always have to be a "sacrifice" or "cost," it could also be their willingness to prioritize DEI among other business goals. *How much does Diversity, Equity and Inclusion Cost?* in Part 2 explores the financial and non-financial costs of implementing successful DEI work.

PART 2:
UNDERSTANDING WHAT IT TAKES

In the last part, I explained how DEI fits within the workplace. Now, let's try to understand what is needed for a successful approach to DEI. This includes resourcing (staff and budget), leadership buy-in and stakeholders who are willing to contribute. This part of the book explores all of these necessities and why they are so critical for success. But first, let's look at this from the opposite perspective and discuss what can go wrong.

Why does DEI work fail?

I've sadly seen so many organizations struggle with their approach to DEI. Typically, there are good intentions all around, but there is something lacking with the execution, resourcing or mindset. It's painful to watch because often it's hard-working employees striving for change who clash with painful realities within their organization. These failures are difficult lessons to learn because they result in wasted time and demotivation and can even damage the organization's credibility. Here are the common reasons why DEI work in organizations fails and how to find a path towards success.

1. Lack of top-down, executive-level endorsement

Often companies see DEI work as either a grassroots (bottom-up) initiative or an isolated initiative within HR. These approaches do not have the necessary executive-level endorsement needed for success. The most successful DEI approaches I've seen have frequent and visible top-down support and endorsement from the most senior people in the organization such as the executive team or senior leadership team. This sends the message that DEI is a topic for the *entire* organization, not just Employee Resource Groups or HR. Without this endorsement, it's challenging for DEI teams to make meaningful progress because stakeholders and employees don't see the topic as a *priority*. To succeed, you will need many strategically positioned leaders that are bought in and willing to put their time, energy and visibility behind the work.

Instead, try this: Before embarking on the work, make sure someone from the leadership team is sponsoring the DEI work, willing to speak about it frequently and champion it within the organization. DEI should be communicated as a strategic priority ranked alongside other critical business priorities. Finally, make sure many leaders across the organization are willing to have a visible role in the DEI journey, such as serving as an executive sponsor of an ERG.

2. Underfunding and underprioritizing

Many companies see hiring for a DEI Director role or setting up a DEI team as the *solution* to their "DEI challenges" because it is a visible step that shows they care about the work. However, it's not the solution. It's the *start* of the solution. If an organization does not adequately fund and staff the team and prioritize their work to achieve their objectives, there will be no progress.

Instead, try this: Before committing to taking on the DEI responsibility as part of your existing job or accepting a job offer for a DEI role, ask the organization how your work will be resourced (including budget and staff). Then take the time to properly understand the challenge ahead of you, with input from stakeholders and employees. Once you can put a strategy in place, be sure the leadership team has signed it off. (See Part 3: *How to create your organization's first DEI strategy*). To make sure you can actually achieve the strategy, tie your budget and staff request to the initiatives in the strategy. If the organization is unwilling to offer budget and staff to make the strategy successful, you can consider scaling back on the scope of the strategy. But it's also possible that your organization may not be interested in the actual work it takes to drive organizational change.

3.   Unrealistic expectations

It's easy to be overly optimistic (to ourselves and our stakeholders) and build up unrealistic expectations about DEI work in the workplace. This is especially true when we look towards activism work in grassroots and nonprofit organizations in our communities for inspiration. We want to see a drastic, speedy change but that's very difficult in large organizations. Organizations are machines. They have their own culture, hierarchy, baggage and skeletons in the closet. It takes time for organizations to change, and most importantly, the organization must *want* to change.

Instead, try this: When planning timelines or deliverables for new projects, make sure you've thought through which stakeholders are needed for your success. And consider what other barriers exist, for example, before promising an ambitious hiring target, make sure you can measure progress and your organization is willing to put the time and processes in place to achieve it.

4. Working without a strategic focus

DEI has a million topics you can focus on at any given moment. You will get whiplash if you constantly change focus and react to incoming requests by starting new projects or initiatives. This reactionary approach makes it very difficult to stay focused and protect the work you are already doing.

Instead, try this: Make sure your DEI work is driven by a holistic, long-term strategy with a roadmap of initiatives that help achieve that strategy. Share the strategy with your stakeholders so they know exactly what you are trying to achieve. To make your work even more transparent and visible to everyone, have a roadmap that is accessible so they can see what's in progress and the status of each initiative. This transparent approach combined with a commitment to not change or increase the scope of the strategy helps protect you from interrupting your work with new ideas or projects or taking on more than you can actually achieve.

5. Failure to acknowledge and address structural issues

Diversity, equity and inclusion work does not exist in a vacuum separate from other workplace processes. It's all interlinked. If your organization has problematic, discriminatory or exclusionary policies or processes, you will struggle to make an impact because you are likely not addressing the root causes of exclusion and inequity. Here's an example: if employees are very frustrated with lack of pay transparency and pay inequality, but instead of addressing this, you focus on diversity hiring -- the frustration around pay will likely get worse and have a negative impact on your hiring initiative.

Instead, try this: Take the time to review processes across the board including hiring, promotions, compensation, succession management, company culture, ethics, healthcare, parental leave and benefits with an eye towards equity to figure out where your problems truly lie. Listen to employees who voice complaints on these processes, their experiences provide important insight. If you have structural issues that need to be addressed, focus on these as your number one priority.

6. Inability to measure or recognize success

DEI work can feel painstaking and slow. In this type of work, specifically, success is not always obvious. Projects can take months to coordinate and launch and then the impact is rarely immediately apparent. It's easy to become disheartened when you are not able to see or measure your success.

Instead, try this: Develop metrics that you track regularly. Make sure the metrics are meaningful and communicated with your stakeholders. These metrics should measure the *impact* of your work. Depending on what you are trying to achieve, metrics may be measured by hiring or attrition data or answers to questions about inclusion, belonging and fairness in a regular survey. In Part 3 of this book, we'll explore *How to measure the impact of your work.*

In general, make sure to acknowledge and celebrate the launch of new projects or initiatives. Of course, there is always more work to be done, but organizational change only happens through slow and steady work over a long period of time.

Yes, there are many ways to struggle with DEI work, but there's not just one way to succeed. I've tried to keep these common pitfalls in mind throughout the book while offering practical approaches that have a good chance of success. But this is a good moment for a reminder. Not everything is within our control. As you saw above, many of the critical elements needed for success lie in the hands of decision-makers or the structure of your organization. We simply cannot control everything, and in some rare cases, success in DEI can be entirely out of reach of the individuals responsible for it. But this book is all about understanding what is *within* our control and how we can set ourselves up for success as best as possible.

What do DEI teams do every day?

Especially if you are embarking on this journey for the first time, it's helpful to understand what a DEI professional or DEI team typically does and how their efforts support a more diverse, equitable and inclusive organization.

What stakeholders *think* DEI teams do

Before we go into the primary responsibilities of DEI teams, let's talk about what stakeholders and employees *think* DEI teams do and why that does not always align with reality. I've found there can be a pretty significant misalignment among stakeholders of what is and isn't the responsibility of the DEI team.

Here are the most common misconceptions I've found of what a DEI team does:

- Language police ready to censor and sanction any inappropriate or "non-PC" language
- Grievance office for all complaints, whether they are related to DEI or not
- Manager of an endless (imaginary) fund for all donation and sponsorship requests
- Personal champion of all employee concerns and requests
- Figurehead to rubber-stamp any policy and communication with a DEI seal of approval

That list is entirely inspired by conversations I had with stakeholders who had precisely those expectations. If you were actually responsible for all of that, it would be impossible to get anything done. So how to deal with this and how to set the *correct* expectations? First, be open and authentic to your stakeholders about what you and your team are responsible for, what your strategy is and what you have the capacity to influence beyond that. Be transparent about who the decision-makers are for DEI-related work. I've often found that some critical DEI topics may structurally fall outside the scope of the DEI team and be difficult to influence, such as pay equity or promotion transparency. Finally, give practical suggestions to employees and leaders for how they can contribute to the DEI work (on this topic, see Part 6: *Deep Dive: Creating Inclusion in the Workplace*).

Now we've covered the misconceptions of DEI work, let's talk about what *is* typically part of the job. Responsibilities and scope will vary from team to team, especially based on their scope or where they are located within the organization. These are the main functions I've observed of typical DEI teams:

Setting the strategy

The most important part of the work of a DEI team is to set the DEI strategy for the organization in coordination with key stakeholders including the leadership team and then regularly communicate progress. The DEI strategy is the guiding light that helps the team prioritize, schedule their work and create their budget. It is, to put it simply, the critical *first* step. (Read more: Part 3: *How to create your organization's first DEI strategy?*).

Implementing the strategy

Typically, the day-to-day tasks of the DEI team are focused on putting their strategy into place by driving initiatives and programs that support the overall goals of the strategy. So, what does this practically look like? Typical activities for a DEI team include:

- Scoping, developing and implementing new DEI programs such as mentorship or inclusive leadership training in line with the strategy
- Meeting with stakeholders and Employee Resource Groups to discuss current and future projects to get their insight and buy-in
- Tracking progress by measuring the success of initiatives and providing regular updates to employees and stakeholders

- Meeting with teams across the organization to talk about their role in supporting DEI

- Driving thought leadership by communicating internally about important milestones, interesting articles and opportunities to learn about DEI

Advising in difficult situations

On top of the strategic work of the DEI team, invariably, some crisis (internal or external) will arise and the DEI team will be called upon to advise on the best course of action. These requests often come with little or no warning and require a lot of urgent time investment. Here are some tangible examples of these situations:

- A tweet sent by your company that uses an ableist slur

- A manager fumbles a Q&A with employees on the topic of gender equity in the workplace

The function of the DEI team in these situations is to quickly advise on how to address these situations. This sometimes includes preparing communication, implementing training or arranging focus groups. The most important thing is to recognize these situations as opportunities to ask ourselves: *Why did this happen?* Instead of just addressing these crises in a reactionary way, take the time to understand the root cause and address it. The best outcome is to put processes in place to prevent a similar situation from happening again in the future.

Supporting leaders to be role models

A crucial role of the DEI team is to support leaders to have the tools, language and confidence to speak about DEI across the organization. For DEI to succeed within an organization, it cannot just be touted from one single team or from the ERGs. It must feel *embedded* in the organization and communication at all levels. Supporting leaders to be active role models is worth the time and energy investment of the DEI team because it empowers them to support your organization's DEI work with their visibility and championing. It also has the added benefit of helping leaders avoid making mistakes when they speak on the fly such as using the wrong language or being unaware of your DEI strategy and priorities.

Harassment and discrimination reporting

In most situations I've seen, the responsibility to develop and implement harassment and discrimination reporting processes (such as a Speak Up System) falls outside the scope of the DEI team. This approach makes sense because, in my view, DEI is less of a compliance topic and more of a change management topic. But nevertheless, there are some DEI teams that are responsible for developing, implementing and managing a discrimination reporting process. This responsibility involves putting a process in place that allows employees, customers and partners to confidentially or anonymously submit incidences where they have experienced or witnessed discrimination. Once the process is in place, the task becomes monitoring submissions and following up on them. Sometimes an ombudsman, an independent and impartial person tasked with looking into complaints, is appointed.

Even if the DEI team is not responsible for discrimination reporting process, it's important to be connected to the team that is to understand patterns of exclusionary or discriminatory behaviors within your organization. This will influence your strategy and help identify the root cause of issues like poor retention and lack of psychological safety.

Who owns DEI?

We've discussed the different types of work DEI teams do, now let's talk about *ownership*. For DEI to succeed, there needs to be a strong sense of ownership across the organization, especially from leadership. It cannot be perceived as a topic that is just owned by a single employee or team, is only relevant to HR or is driven solely by Employee Resource Groups. Let me illustrate this: A few years ago, I talked to a friend about her new role. In addition to her day job, she had recently taken responsibility for

DEI at the small investment fund where she worked. She was hosting internal and external events to showcase the importance of diverse founders and an inclusive ecosystem for successful investments. After several events, she had a conversation with a partner at the fund. The partner referred to DEI as *her* topic that she was solely responsible for. She replied: "DEI is not *my* topic. It is *your* topic and the *fund's* topic. If you can't see how this work touches everything we do, then you are missing the value this work has for our fund." She decided to stop working on DEI because the leadership team didn't see it as a priority and was unwilling to accept any personal responsibility for it. They saw it only as her "pet project." This perception does a lot of damage to the work we are trying to do. It's difficult to get other stakeholders on board to support DEI work if they don't see a commitment or ownership across the organization.

In the next section, we'll explore what commitments (budget, staffing, visibility and prioritization) are necessary for the success of DEI work.

How much does Diversity, Equity and Inclusion cost?

"What is a reasonable budget for my DEI team?" This is an interesting question to try to answer. It seems pretty straightforward, but let's step back from the task of estimating budgets and think about the broader costs of DEI beyond invoices and credit card statements. By broader costs, I'm referring to the time, energy, staffing and visibility that DEI requires to succeed. All of this has a cost in some way or another. Ironically, I've found that budget may be the easiest to secure among all of these costs. The other costs are much more expensive because they force an organization to make tough decisions on prioritization, revise their processes or adjust their goals. These costs are much more complex and more challenging to estimate. Nevertheless, they are necessary for success.

But before we explore more, let's address how DEI is often discussed. I often hear discussion around the ROI (Return on Investment) of DEI. Leaders often ask: "What's the business case for DEI? How much money will it save us or make us?" For a decade, consulting firms have been touting the message that DEI makes businesses money through innovation and other means.[1] Some leaders want to hear this argument in order to feel convinced that they should *invest* in DEI. But this is a slippery slope. When a DEI team must constantly demonstrate how they have saved or made their company money, it forces their measure of success to be quantifiably financial. The reality is that it is very difficult to quantify all the ways that DEI initiatives increase productivity, improve retention, attract better talent, help build better products and connect with your customers. And frankly, some DEI initiatives will result in no profit or budget saved, but that doesn't mean they aren't worth doing.

So, if an executive team is not convinced that DEI is a critical strategic initiative of their organization (unless it saves them money), then they are not fully bought in. When the executive team isn't bought in, it's very difficult to make tangible progress.

I'd suggest a different framing around this ROI narrative. Instead of asking how DEI will save your organization money, I'd ask senior leaders:

> *What kind of company do you want to build? How does Diversity, Equity and Inclusion fit into that company?*
>
> *Is the company you want to build a diverse company?*
>
> *Is the culture of that company welcoming and inclusive?*
>
> *What kind of testimonials do you want to see in glassdoor[2] reviews?*

---

[1]McKinsey, 2020. *Diversity wins: How inclusion matters.*
https://www.mckinsey.com/featured-insights/diversity-and-inclusion/diversity-wins-how-inclusion-matters

[2]Glassdoor is a website where current and former employees anonymously review companies: https://www.glassdoor.com

This is not meant to pressure leaders into a particular way of thinking. Honestly, it's a very personal choice based on one's own values. I'm just trying to shift the conversation from the ROI of DEI to a more personal decision of how a founder or executive team wants to run their organization and how DEI fits into that vision.

Now, back to the question of *What does DEI cost?* This is a complex question. When you think about the cost of DEI, it's not just the budget. It's the entire cost of an authentic, strategic approach to DEI. This includes budget, hiring or allocating staff, the cost of revising processes, the cost of collaboration across stakeholders and most importantly, the cost of prioritizing DEI alongside or in place of other strategic initiatives. Here are some of the costs, both obvious and not-so-obvious, required for the success of DEI:

Leadership buy-in

I mentioned this before but let me reiterate: Support from the leadership team is absolutely necessary for the success of DEI work. In particular, I've found it very helpful to have one or two DEI executive champions that are ultimately responsible for DEI. In order to give the proper importance to DEI efforts, the champions should be willing to put their time, energy and visibility behind the work. This functions as an executive endorsement and ensures that employees throughout the organization also consider DEI to have high strategic importance. Ideally, this also pulls DEI away from a purely HR domain and sets it alongside other business-critical efforts. Having an executive champion also role models inclusive behavior to other executives and offers them a peer to call on for advice.

What does this cost? The time of an executive is expensive, of course. But also, their time is finite. They can only focus on so many topics at once. When they focus some of their time on DEI, it means they are not focusing on something else, so this comes with a cost. This cost varies depending on many things but will be highest during times of crisis. In terms of crisis, I refer to any situation requiring immediate attention and response to handle a difficult situation. These situations can take up massive amounts of time, which pulls the executive away from anything else they may have been focusing on.

An additional cost associated with an effective executive champion is the time and energy they need to develop their awareness and understanding of DEI. This empowers them to speak about it confidently and competently. The DEI team plays an important role here, but often an executive coach is needed for this.

What to do if you find yourself without an executive champion? First define how you want this champion to support you in your work and what time commitment and skills are required. Then simply ask members of the executive team to see who would be interested.

Hiring or allocating staff resources for a DEI team

For a smaller organization (less than 1,000 employees), it may be possible to kick off DEI by allocating responsibilities to existing staff, such as 50 percent of an existing employee's role (an HR project manager, for example). For a larger organization, it's important that there is clear ownership of DEI with a dedicated role or team.

The correct positioning of the DEI team is another crucial element of success. Sometimes a DEI role is positioned three or four levels away from the executive team, each level adding more bureaucratic hierarchy to manage and mangle the efforts. In the worst-case scenario, intermediary managers function as knowledge gatekeepers between the DEI team and important decision-makers. This arrangement gives the impression to stakeholders that the work of the DEI team is not actually a priority. When setting up a team for the first time, my recommendation is always to have the role or team report as directly as possible into the executive team. This also means they would have a clear line of communication and a trustworthy relationship with the executive team. This creates the situation where members of the executive team feel comfortable to reach out directly when they have questions or need guidance.

How much does this cost? Salaries vary widely globally, so check around for locally relevant information. But in general, I have found that hiring for DEI roles will typically cost companies more than they were planning to spend. Perhaps this is because they haven't researched the industry (which is constantly growing, and DEI professionals are always in very high demand) or perceive the work to be in line with more junior roles such as HR managers or generalists.

The proper positioning of a DEI role or team within an organizational structure can also have a cost. It may require the restructuring of teams or challenge a very hierarchical system, potentially hurting some egos in the process. I've seen a lot of organizations bury the DEI team in three or more levels of HR organizational hierarchy or have the sole DEI role report to someone who is not at all knowledgeable about DEI and unwilling to let the DEI team work directly with decision-makers. This ultimately hurts the chances of the team to build credible and influential relationships with senior stakeholders. These relationships are important for the success of DEI work because they help get executives on board and champion the work you are doing, often in channels you wouldn't have access to otherwise.

Supporting staff resources

No DEI initiative will ever exist in a vacuum with no external or stakeholder dependencies. DEI work, by nature, tries to address inequality and exclusion in the structures and systems of the workplace. Because of this, the work *must* be in collaboration with many, many stakeholders. These stakeholders are critical to the success of your DEI efforts. This includes HR professionals (learning & development roles, business partners, performance management, data analysts), communication professionals (internal and external), the events team, legal and compliance professionals, and many more.

These stakeholders need to recognize DEI as a strategic priority and be willing to support it with their working time. This perception that DEI is a priority will not happen accidentally, it needs to be purposefully communicated top-down. Everyone from the executive team down to the managers of your stakeholders need to perceive DEI work as a priority, not a passion project or an add-on. If you constantly struggle to get the necessary stakeholder support you need, then ultimately, it will be difficult for your work to be successful because it is not recognized as important.

What does this collaboration look like? Practically this looks like a communication professional supporting internal DEI communication, an HR data analyst providing reports on employee retention and attrition or a legal team advising on GDPR for diversity data collection.

How much does this cost? When this collaboration works well, stakeholders will support DEI work as requested. This can vary in time from a few hours a week to longer periods, depending on the project. When stakeholders support the DEI work, it means they will have less time for something else. For example, a data analyst supporting the DEI team to provide reporting and analysis on a quarterly basis may need to de-prioritize another internal request. Often, this *cost* lies in the willingness of managers of these teams to commit to collaborating and supporting the DEI work and making sure it's important among other competing priorities.

Supporting Employee Resource Groups

What about the work of Employee Resource Groups? Organizers often put in several hours of work per week building their communities and working collaboratively with the organization. When thinking about budgeting or resources, what's the best way to account for this time? Many organizations unfortunately consider this purely volunteer work (to be done in employees' "free time"). But this work positively contributes to the work culture and is often used in external communication to showcase an inclusive working environment in order to attract new employees. Out of respect for the energy and effort of ERG organizers and considering what the organization gains from these contributions, it makes sense for this work to be properly recognized *as work*, not volunteer time.

How much does this cost? Many organizations have policies where employees can spend a set percentage of their work on research side-projects or personal learning and development. In the same vein, a policy for ERG organizers to spend some percent of their working time on ERG-related activities supports their time and acknowledges this work *as work*. This has a practical cost because an ERG organizer's working capacity is reduced. Especially if there are several ERG organizers within one team, it may make sense to add an additional role to cover the same amount of work or equitably adjust responsibilities within the team. In Part 4: *Everything about Employee Resource Groups* I provide a lot of explanation on how to set ERGs up for success and recognize and reward their work.

Process changes

Changing internal processes is another substantial cost to account for. The work of a DEI team often focuses on improving or creating new processes that try to address structural inequality or exclusion. These processes lead to positive changes in the organization but often require a lot of coordination and buy-in to successfully implement. A few examples:

- developing new processes to address and reduce bias in hiring or promotion processes
- establishing a policy to ensure governing bodies or committees are diverse
- introducing an inclusive language policy as a standard in the organization

Developing these processes is just step 1. Actually implementing them and ensuring compliance is step 2 through infinity. Let's explore a practical example: The DEI team develops an HR Diversity Recruiting

Checklist[3] to support better, less biased decision making during the hiring process, ideally to result in increased diversity in new hires. But simply developing the checklist is just step 1. The crucial part is making sure all hiring managers use the checklist by tracking its use and then further developing it based on feedback. The latter requires much more investment, stakeholder buy-in and ongoing monitoring. This is where the bulk of the work actually lies.

What does this cost? Let's use the above example. To make sure this is really adopted, you will need top-down communication to show that this new process is necessary and mandatory. This has a cost because it requires buy-in and visibility from senior leaders. It may require deprioritizing another initiative to prioritize this one. Once the new process is adopted, it may result in slower hiring because hiring managers need to follow additional steps. This could be expensive in terms of lost productivity for a team that wants to grow rapidly. It could also result in the need to increase salaries to attract talent from diverse communities or utilizing new job boards (which have a cost). There are many not-so-obvious costs hidden behind what seems like a relatively straightforward and "low cost" initiative. The trust cost comes in the implementation, not just the development.

If your organization is not willing to accept the cost of putting new processes in place, it's incredibly difficult to actually make change. Without allies high up in the organization that champion the new processes and encourage adoption, it's impossible to put them in place.

Budget

Now back to the question people always want to know: *How big should the DEI budget be?* This is difficult to answer, and it can vary drastically. When estimating your budget, not including salaries, first start with your strategy. Once your strategy is created and aligned with the leadership

---

[3]For more information on Diversity Recruiting Checklists, check out Part 5: *Launching a holistic diversity hiring program.*

team, your budget estimates should be linked directly to programs and initiatives that are in your strategy. It should also be clear what impact or outcome you are trying to achieve with each expense.

There is a lot of variability in DEI budgets depending on the scope of strategy (internal vs. external), organization size, industry and location. It's difficult to say what a "typical" budget is. For example, tech companies will likely spend much more on DEI because they have a more significant challenge recruiting and are often combating biased or even toxic work environments.[4] But we can make some general estimates. "A recent study released by the Society of Human Resource Management (SHRM) reported diversity-department budgets at Fortune 1000 companies average around $1.5 million per year. The range for diversity department budgets was $30,000 to $5.1 million. When diversity was housed in Human Resources, the average annual diversity budget was $239,000".[5]

It's important to put those estimates into context: Fortune 1000 companies have an average workforce size of 34,000 and average revenue of 15 billion.[6] So they are quite a bit larger than the companies likely trying to figure out what their (first) DEI budget should be. For organizations with 2,000–10,000 employees who are just beginning their DEI journey, I'd estimate a starting budget of somewhere between 50,000 and 300,000[7] euros not including salaries. There is a lot of variability here so I'm providing these numbers only as a benchmark.

----

[4]Tech Industry Gender Inequality Report, November 4, 2021 | Kerry (Rosvold) Peters: *https://getyournewview.com/tech-industry-gender-inequality/*

[5]*Diversity Inclusion Budgets.* Diversity Best Practices, 2020.
https://www.diversitybestpractices.com/sites/diversitybestpractices.com/files/attachments/2020/11/updated_budgets_2020_0.pdf

[6]Data source: *https://www.someka.net/excel-template/fortune-1000-excel-list/*

[7]These estimates are based on my experience working in DEI in Germany. The estimates are in Euros, relevant for EU based companies. I haven't found standard benchmarks for DEI budgets for EU companies widely available. Likely, these figures will become out-of-date quickly as companies regularly increase their commitment and therefore budgets for DEI.

Here's a rough distribution of a sample DEI budget that supports an internally focused DEI strategy:

- Budget provided to Employee Resource Groups (2,000-5,000 per ERG): 10,000–50,000 euros
- Training development and implementation for employees including unconscious bias, anti-racism, inclusive leadership: 30,000-150,000 euros
- Other DEI initiatives including working with external consultants or advisors: 10,000-50,000 euros
- Partnerships with community organizations: 5,000-50,000 euros
- Recruiting and Branding including posting on job boards, attending conferences for recruiting: 10,000-30,000 euros

Budget costs will greatly depend on whether you are managing projects internally (such as developing an inclusive leadership program in-house) or are working with external vendors and consultants which can have daily rates anywhere between 1,000 and 5,000 euros.

One thing I'm absolutely sure about: it makes no sense for a DEI team in a for-profit organization to be expected to function with ZERO budget. And in some ways, the amount of budget allocated is an indication of how important the organization perceives the topic. With that said, do not be discouraged if your organization has only a small budget for DEI. More money does not always mean more impact. Much can be achieved with a combination of leadership buy-in and willingness across the organization to prioritize DEI. Managing a smaller budget simply boils down to strategically allocating money to projects that have the most impact.

Final thoughts on the cost of DEI

In many ways, the cost of DEI is much higher than just the total of salaries and budgets because it really requires an organization to grapple with *why* it does things and *can* it actually change. But the benefits of a well-executed DEI strategy are also higher than what can be calculated on a spreadsheet. Much of the DEI work we do has an incalculable benefit: avoiding future mistakes and disasters. Many, many brands[8] have had crises in the past few years, likely not because of malicious behavior but because of lack of education and awareness on racism, equity and inclusion in general. It's difficult to realistically factor this risk avoidance into cost calculations, though some have tried.[9] These intangible costs and benefits underline the futility of making a financial justification for DEI. In the end, prioritizing DEI must be a conscious, morally driven decision top-down and not just because of the financials.

What skills are most useful for a DEI role?

We've talked about what DEI costs, now the next question becomes what skills are needed. Surprisingly, in Europe, many people I've talked to over the years found themselves in a DEI role or leading on a DEI strategy because they were simply *appointed* to do so. Typically, they had a project management role within HR or were simply passionate about the topic. Even with good intentions all around, it's very easy to enter this situation feeling unprepared and ill-equipped.

First, why do organizations tend to nominate someone internally and put them in charge of such a critical topic? Based on my experience, I have a few conclusions:

1. Organizations feel the need to make a visible commitment, but they are unwilling to make the financial investment of hiring a seasoned DEI professional and would rather put someone internal on the task *first*.

---

[8]H&M: *https://www.nytimes.com/2018/01/08/business/hm-monkey.html*
VW: *https://www.bbc.com/news/business-52733444*
Nivea: *https://www.nytimes.com/2017/04/04/business/media/nivea-ad-online-uproar-racism.html*
[9]Understanding the Costs of Harassment Prevention and DEI Training
https://businesslawtoday.org/2021/05/11941/

2. Organizations tried and failed to hire externally because DEI professionals are in high demand and can request high salaries that are beyond the planned budget.

3. Organizations greatly underestimate the amount of expertise, financial investment and culture change necessary to drive effective DEI work.

4. Organizations simply don't take the topic seriously and want a quick solution, regardless of whether it is a *good* solution.

Sometimes the reason is a messy combination of everything above. Regardless of what's behind this decision, it is possible to make some positive change even if you and your organization have just started on this journey.

Let's take a deep dive into the skills that are most useful for a DEI role (according to my own experience) and how to build them. Everyone has a different approach to DEI work, and everyone brings a different skillset, so take this with a reasonably big handful of salt.

Communication

The ability to communicate your work, including both basic and complex DEI concepts, to your colleagues and stakeholders is really important. This is especially true because the people you work with will have a very wide range of understanding of DEI, so you need to find a way to communicate successfully to everyone no matter where they are coming from. Also, it's very important to be able to present various arguments about why DEI is or should be a priority — different people are convinced in different ways.

How to build this skill? Try to write your own explanations of different DEI concepts. Practice explaining these concepts to friends and family. As inspiration, find resources online that successfully communicate in easily understandable ways. Remember, your audience members do not have PhDs in gender studies or intercultural communication. You need to make these topics accessible to them. Ask for direct feedback about whether your explanations were clear and informative. If you have colleagues who work in internal communications, try to get advice from them. The book *On Writing Well* by William Zinsser is also a great resource. It has practical advice on communicating (through writing) in a clear, precise and authentic way.

Project Management

Your DEI strategy is not valuable unless you can deliver on its commitments which requires project management skills. This includes breaking a project into definable and measurable tasks and tracking its progress to completion. It is also essential that your key stakeholders have transparency on the status of your work and know what they are responsible for.

How to build this skill? Learn more about the basics of project management through tutorials on YouTube or your favorite learning platform. Try out different project management tools[10] to find what you like best.

Stakeholder Management

A lot of DEI work is "herding cats," meaning getting people across your organization in different roles (HR, Communications, Technology, Legal, Corporate Social Responsibility, ERG organizers) to compromise and work together. In general, it's all about finding a solution that is a win or near-win for everyone. This involves a lot of delicate stakeholder management, smoothing over misunderstandings and creating moments of empathy across differences. Specifically, it's important to get everyone on board with what you are trying to accomplish and address any concerns they may have. To do this, it's helpful to take time to fully understand your stakeholders' individual motivations and hesitations. I

---

[10]Project management tools: Trello, Jira, or Asana

often think of this as brokering compromises -- this typically takes a lot of work but sadly doesn't always feel very satisfying.

How to build this skill? This is a tough one to build because you really learn this in practice and by making mistakes (and then learning from them). Before you kick off a project, make a stakeholder map with three categories:

- Collaborative (stakeholders whose contributions are integral to the success of the project)

- Consultative (stakeholders who should be invited to provide their insight and feedback)

- Informative (stakeholders who only need to be informed and aware of the project)

This map will be an important reminder of who is critical to the success of your project. Next, engage your stakeholders early in your project and make sure they feel like they have a personal stake in the work. As you move ahead with your project and are keeping your stakeholders engaged, ask for feedback on whether they feel sufficiently informed and build on this feedback. I've found it better to over-inform stakeholders than under-inform.

DEI Best Practices

Understanding DEI Best practices and getting inspired by the work of others in the industry is crucial. By DEI best practices, I'm referring to an understanding of common concepts[11] in DEI but also what initiatives or projects will be most effective for the goals you are trying to achieve in your strategy. It's impossible to know every right answer for every situation. A more important skill is to know *how to find the right answer.* Your stakeholders recognize you as an expert and will come to you with a variety of DEI questions on any number of topics (for example: *How*

---

[11]DEI Glossary of terms can be helpful in building this knowledge, such as:
https://seramount.com/research-insights/glossary-diversity-equity-and-inclusion

can we make this meeting room more accessible? How should we label a gender-inclusive bathroom? How can the cafeteria be more inclusive for different religious diets?) The real skill becomes *how* to research these topics and synthesize information from various sources to reach a conclusion. Remember to consult experts and people who are part of the communities affected by these recommendations to find the right answers.

How to build this skill? This is another skill best built on the job but developing a list of trusted resources and a network of peers you can reach out to in these situations really helps. Your Employee Resource Groups also have a lot of first-hand knowledge that can be very useful when answering questions that are relevant to their communities. Another way to build this skill is to research some sample questions such as: *What should a gender transitioning guide for your workplace cover? What are important considerations when setting up prayer rooms?* Try to find a variety of sources and synthesize the information into a short proposal. In reality, it's hard to predict what questions you will get on the job. The best approach I've found is to be curious and open to learning from experts and high-quality resource materials instead of guessing or assuming based on limited knowledge.

Setting Boundaries

In DEI, more than other professional fields, you'll need to set boundaries on how much of yourself (meaning your time, energy and emotions) you can invest in your job. It's easy to get wrapped up in the goals you are trying to achieve and the individual experiences of your colleagues and overcommit and then burn out. This is especially true for people who are working in DEI and are a part of marginalized communities. The work becomes even more personal. Our own motivations and values also make it difficult to set the correct boundaries and emotional distance between us and the role. Nevertheless, it's impossible to fix every problem, especially because many of them will fall outside your control.

How to build this skill: Proactively set boundaries of how much you are willing to commit to the work. I've found reducing my working days, consciously planning to not read email outside of work hours and mentally unplugging on my days off to be helpful for me. Take care to develop the awareness to know when you need a break or time off. Generally, try to understand what is under your control and within the scope of your role and what is not. And importantly, don't be afraid to communicate to your stakeholders about what you cannot accomplish. Saying *no* is often part of the job.

Final thoughts on skills

You may be surprised that I didn't list *passion for DEI* among the top skills for a DEI professional to succeed in their role. Of course, it's important to care about the work you do. But it's also essential to set boundaries and differentiate between the topics you are personally passionate about and what you can realistically accomplish in a workplace.

I've found that it is easy to idealize DEI jobs. In theory, they give you the chance to work on a topic you are deeply passionate about and make meaningful change. The meaningful change part is definitely possible, but I personally don't think the work feels like activism in the way that grassroots community organizing does. For me, it's more about slow and sometimes tedious organizational change while getting stakeholders (who have a variety of opinions on DEI) on board. I want to be candid about the reality of the work because it can be easy to be disappointed. Setting the right expectations from the beginning helps you find satisfaction in the work.

How to hire a DEI consultant

If your organization is not yet ready to hire a full-time DEI professional, a consultant can help you figure out what your organization needs, set up a strategy or implement an initiative such as a survey. Even if you do have a DEI team in place, a consultant can contribute much needed expertise and outside perspective to make your team more impactful.

Working with a good consultant can unlock doors for you. But, if it goes wrong, it can be a massive waste of time for everyone involved and not deliver what you were hoping for. Whether you are looking for a consultant to design a series of trainings or someone to help you create your first DEI strategy, here's everything you need to know about working with a consultant.[12]

What to expect from working with a consultant?

Think about this relationship as a two-way street. Yes, you are hoping to hire someone to do consulting work for you and you will be vetting them, but they are also vetting you. There is often a power imbalance when one company is employing another, but don't forget, a good consultant has limited time and capacity. They will prioritize their time on clients that are a good match for them. Likely in your first few interactions, they are assessing whether you as a client and your project are a good fit and whether they have the capacity and expertise to complete it. Being aware of this dynamic is essential. So, what is the process of working with a consultant?

Typically, as someone wishing to hire a consultancy, you will reach out to potential consultants via email or their website. First, you share some basic information about the project you want to start. The next step is to have a meeting where you discuss the project and budget. Following that meeting and after clearing up any open questions, you both decide whether you wish to proceed. If so, the consultant then sends you a formal quote to review. This is essentially a budget proposal that includes the scope of the project and deliverables. This phase of the process can take several weeks (or longer) depending on the backlog of the consultant and any additional information you need to gather on your side before fully scoping your project.

---

[12]Floria Moghimi, one of the feedback readers for this book, inspired and collaborated on this section. Through Floria's DEI consulting business (*https://floriamoghimi.de/en*), she has met hundreds of DEI practitioners and organizations hoping to implement DEI. Her insight and expertise has been a welcomed addition to the book.

Depending on your location and the dependencies of the work, the next steps may be a bit different. If you accept the proposal, it may be as simple as agreeing via email to begin the work. But for some cases, you may need to formally sign a contract or exchange other legal documents such as NDAs. Essentially this step commits both sides to the budget, planned scope of work, deliverables, timelines, obligations, and other legal stuff. The work doesn't begin until this happens.

Regarding timelines, typically, a consultant has many concurrent projects, and yours will need to fit in with the others in their queue. This may mean it will not get immediate attention and the timeline may not meet your expectations. Additionally, if there is anything from your side necessary for the consultant to begin the work (such as data, interviews or internal research), the timelines will be delayed until you deliver this.

Make sure it's clear with the consultant, who is the single point of contact, so they know how to get in touch. While the consultant is working on your project, expect to be an active and available participant. They may need introductions to others in your organization or to discuss some aspects of the project. You may be asked to give feedback on interim deliverables or participate in planning sessions. This collaboration is part of a successful project. You should plan to be available as requested during the project through to its delivery.

Depending on the duration and scope of the project, you will likely be invoiced monthly, or in other cases, only when the project is completed. Each invoice you receive has a deadline for payment that needs to be met or the project may be delayed.

What to do before you reach out?

1. Get the mandate to lead the work

Consultants sometimes get contacted by someone who has the ambition to work on a DEI project, but they haven't yet been granted the mandate within their organization to lead this work. This could be a member of a Works Council or ERG or just an interested employee. Unfortunately, though well-intentioned, this can create a false start when the decision-maker is not a part of the evaluation and selection process. By decision-maker, I mean the person ultimately responsible for funding the project and deciding which consultant to work with. Before you begin the process, make sure you have the mandate to hire a consultant, you've identified a project lead and have a budget allocated. Consider these prerequisites to starting your outreach.

2.   Have the right people in the room at the first meeting

As mentioned above, the decision-maker is crucial. If that is not you, make sure you invite the decision-maker. Their involvement from the beginning makes sure that you are using the time you have with the consultant as efficiently as possible. If there is another critical stakeholder whose contributions are absolutely necessary, make sure they are there as well. For example, if you have an executive sponsor or managing director that is really engaged in your DEI work, be sure to invite them. Their perspective on how the project fits into their business may be valuable insight. But with that said, this meeting should not be a whole panel of people. Keep it to 2, or maximum 3 at the first meeting. Otherwise, there will likely be lots of discussion and debate among the participants from your side, making the meeting less productive.

3.   Do your research and allocate your budget in advance

Before talking with them, it's impossible to know what a consultant will charge for your project. But you can do some research in advance to understand a ballpark figure. Typically consultants charge either a flat rate for a project or an hourly fee. You can expect an hourly fee to vary from minimally 100 euros per hour to more than 300.[13] What not to do: reach out to a dozen consultants and ask them all for a quote so you can compare. This generates a lot of time and effort for everyone involved,

---

[13] *Diversity Consultant* by Martha Frase-Blunt, June 1, 2004. *https://www.shrm.org/hr-today/news/hr-magazine/Pages/0604agenda_diversity3.aspx*; *What you get when you hire a DEI consultant* by Kiran Herbert, August 5, 2020.
https://www.outsidebusinessjournal.com/issues/diversity-equity-inclusion/miho-aida-q-and-a/

with a low likelihood of success. Floria Moghimi shares: "When you're about to buy a house you set the budget before you start the search. DEI is not that different. Setting the budget in advance saves the consultants you want to work with a lot of time. There are villas, and there are one-bedroom apartments. Decide what you want to build. We're skilled to do both." For more information on the costs of DEI check out Part 2: *How much does Diversity, Equity and Inclusion cost?*

Also, remember: the consultants you work with are humans working in DEI just like you. They deal with the emotional weight of the work while also navigating inequality and systemic barriers in their own lives. Every additional request or meeting before the contract is signed may take one or two hours more of unpaid work. This work is well spent if the project has a good chance of moving ahead. But if there is a slim to zero change of that project ever coming to life, then this is simply a lot of wasted time. Being aware of this and doing research in advance to narrow down your outreach is respectful of their time and energy. Once you have done your research and know your budget, you can focus your outreach to target two or three consultants you think may be the best fit. Sharing your budget with them up front will give them the chance to reply quickly if they are not able to suit your needs.

4. Be open to guidance

You may think you are 100% set on a specific project and how it should be completed. But remember, the consultant has years of experience delivering projects to clients and has seen it go well… and not so well. Sometimes we think we want one thing (for example: unconscious bias training), but we actually need something else. Be open to guidance and consider their advice on what is the best approach for you.

Find the *right* consultant for you

There's a lot to consider when figuring out which consultancy is right for your project. To find someone, you can ask for recommendations from people you trust or search the web. But context matters. Searching for a consultant who has worked in your geographic location or industry is an excellent start because they will more likely understand the specific challenges you are facing. Try to find a consultant willing to step back and think about the bigger picture and the root cause of the challenge you are trying to solve, not just deliver a single training and call it a day. How the culture and style of your organization mesh with the consultant is also important, you want to find someone that you trust and will enjoy working with.

If you are reaching out to a bigger consultancy, clarify upfront with whom you'll be working. Even after your initial meeting, it may not be obvious who will work on your project, and you'll want to consider the experience and seniority levels of the consultants. Some projects and trainings require a higher level of skill and experience. Working with a more senior consultant will likely also come with a higher rate. Be sure to also consider the diversity of the agency itself. Is it a diverse team with lived experience relevant to your project? Are they comfortable and skilled at advising on topics such as anti-racism or microaggressions?

And lastly, think about your own biases, privilege and the diversity of your professional network. This all has a chance to impact who is recommended to you and who you consider working with. Develop standardized criteria (such as a checklist of skills and relevant experience you are hoping for) to evaluate and compare consultancies to give you some perspective and make a better, less biased decision.

Let's cover a few important don'ts:

1. Don't expect the consultant to fix everything, especially fundamental organizational issues. Addressing those types of issues takes a commitment from inside your organization.

2. Don't try to negotiate prices down, though you can likely scale back the scope of the project to fit your budget.

3. Don't expect to sit back and watch - the consultant will need your engagement and input throughout the project.

I hope this guidance can be helpful in thinking about your next project and finding the right consultant for it. Many of the best working relationships are built over time with a high level of trust. Starting the relationship off in the right way will help build that trust quickly and get your project off to a great start.

PART 3:
SETTING UP FOR SUCCESS

In the last section, we talked all about what DEI teams do, what DEI costs and what skills are most relevant. Once you have a good understanding of that, it's time to talk about what pieces you can put in place to set you and your team up for success. This section is all about putting the essential elements in place for a successful approach to DEI.

What is *success* for DEI in the workplace?

Before we talk about the elements leading to success, how does it actually look to succeed in your DEI work for your organization? How you define success will likely depend on many factors like culture, geography and industry. Sadly, there is never one clear goal post to achieve for DEI. In many ways, it's an evolving journey which requires uncovering and addressing challenges along the way. This journey also requires the flexibility and resilience to adapt to the needs of your organization.

Success in DEI must touch on each of the words that make up the acronym: *Diversity*, *Equity* and *Inclusion*. Let's start with *equity*. Earlier in the book, equity is defined as "the fair treatment, access, and opportunity for all people by identifying and eliminating systemic or individual barriers that prevent full participation and engagement of groups and individuals." Working towards equity requires you to look both inside and outside of your organization to understand the barriers that stand in the way. The first step in determining your definition of success regarding equity is to understand the relevant barriers that exist to equity and imagine what it looks like to remove those. Ask yourself: What does your industry look like when you are able to remove barriers for people to access industry-relevant education? What new opportunities are created when you address a lack of networking opportunities necessary to break into the field? How different does your leadership team look once you investigate your promotion process to remove systemic bias that prevent Women of Color from being promoted in their careers? These are the tough questions you need to ask your organization in order to understand what success you are striving for.

What does achieving success in diversity look like? Perhaps this is more tangible than equity. Essentially, look at the diversity around you. This includes the diversity of the geographic areas you operate in or hire from, the diversity of your customer base, the diversity of your broader industry. Success will likely mean that your organization strives to reflect a combination of the diversity around you. Keep in mind, your organization is likely made up of many different roles, functions and seniority levels. How diversity is distributed across your organization is also worth considering. If diversity only exists in one part of the business or only at junior levels, it's difficult to claim success.

What does success in inclusion look like? Is it enough that, on average across your entire organization, the level of engagement, inclusion and belonging is relatively high? Unfortunately, no. When organizations survey employees on engagement, they often look at the average response across everyone in the organization. But sadly, this aggregation of data often obscures and marginalizes the experiences of employees who are in the minority. Their experiences get drowned out by others who do not face discrimination or exclusion. A measure of success for inclusion should be defined not by how the *average* employee feels. Instead, it should be defined as whether your ERG communities or other groups that do not have representation or visibility in leadership feel a sense of inclusion, equity and belonging. This topic is explored more in *Creating an employee inclusion and identity survey* in Part 5.

The most crucial element for setting yourself up for success is an aligned and transparent DEI strategy. But success needs more than just a strategy. Success requires a highly engaged governing body (known as a DEI Council), the ability to measure your progress and ultimately, the need to communicate your work to your stakeholders. We'll cover each of these elements and how to set them up.

How to set up a DEI council

A DEI council is incredibly valuable in kickstarting the DEI work for your organization. A DEI council (sometimes referred to as a steering committee) is the governing body that advises and oversees the DEI work of your organization. *Why create a DEI council?* If you are the only person in your organization that is "responsible" for DEI, the work can be lonely, overwhelming and sometimes fruitless. An effective council serves as a motivated committee that brings direction, endorsement and visibility to your work.

Before even setting up a strategy, it's important first to set up the council. A DEI Council is a diverse and representative group of leaders or experts within your organization. They should be ready to prioritize DEI work, be knowledgeable and open to feedback and be willing to give visibility to DEI in their part of the business or geographic location. Council members should be leaders, but they do not need to be at the very top of the organization. It can sometimes be more effective to prioritize expertise and the ability to dedicate time over seniority when searching for council members.

Creating governance

The governance of the DEI council is the documented purpose, structure and decision making process of the council. This is sometimes known as *Terms of Reference*. Start with lightweight governance. If you spend too much time defining the governance, it cuts into the time you can actually do the work, and it may ultimately be wasted effort if the governance needs changing. Instead, it's helpful to leave room for flexibility to adapt your governance over time. Have a first draft of the governance ready while you are inviting members to join. This allows you to communicate transparent expectations and help invited members of the council make informed decisions about whether they can participate and commit. The following list includes the main elements of DEI council governance and how to define each one.

1. Purpose

This is a statement that outlines why the group exists and what it is tasked to do. To define this, ask yourself: What is the purpose of the group? What is the group meant to do? Is the group meant just to provide guidance or also take ownership of work?

2. Membership and commitment

This is a statement of the eligibility criteria for council members and what their participation commitment should be. To define this, ask yourself: What makes someone eligible to participate? Is there a seniority requirement or an expertise requirement? Are members of Employee Resource Groups invited to participate? What is the commitment required (time, effort and availability)? Is there a rotation of members? Is there a process in which new members are added to the group?

3. Duration

This statement defines how long the council should exist. Ask yourself: Is this group meant to last indefinitely or is there a clear finish line? For example: once the strategy is defined, is the group then dissolved? Defining this also sets expectations among your members, so they know what they are committing to.

4. Meeting frequency and structure

This statement defines how often the council meets and the meeting structure. Ask yourself: How often should the council meet? How long should the meetings be? Because this element will most likely change over time, it's fine to propose an initial meeting structure: such as monthly meetings of 1.5 hours. Set the expectation that council members may need to communicate between meetings.

5. Accessible meetings

Consider how to make the council meetings accessible in their timing and structure. Are you working across time zones and locations? Be sure to find a time that works for everyone, or if that's not possible, try out alternating meeting times. *Inclusive Remote Working* in Part 6 has many tips for setting up inclusive and accessible meetings.

6. Decision making process

This statement defines how decisions are made within the group. Ask yourself: Does everyone have equal voting rights? Do some members have more heavily weighted decision rights due to how the decisions affect their work and responsibilities? Is there a process to revisit or appeal decisions? This doesn't necessarily need to be too formal, but it helps to consider and discuss these questions in advance before you must collaboratively make a decision.

7. Facilitating and chairing the meetings

It's important to identify who prepares the pre-read documentation before the meetings and assembles the agenda, sends invites or takes meeting minutes. This is typically known as the *facilitator*. Secondly, it's important to determine who *chairs* the meeting. This is the person who moderates the meetings and calls for votes or decisions in the meeting. Decide if these roles rotate or if they are assigned to a fixed person or persons. It's possible to have the facilitator role and the chair role held by the same person, but it can be difficult to take minutes during the meeting and also move along the agenda.

8. Working between meetings

Decide whether the DEI council has responsibilities to contribute to the DEI work between meetings or if their role is limited to providing guidance and decision making through their participation in the council meetings. The real amount of work will come after the council is set up, once the implementation of the strategy begins. Sometimes councils have working groups who are accountable for making progress on initiatives between council meetings.

9. Stakeholder mapping

This is a list of all the stakeholders who are critical to the success of the council's work. To define this, create an initial list of stakeholders that must be actively engaged or will be somehow affected by the council's decisions. Keep them informed of the outcomes of the meetings. This list will likely evolve over time as the scope of work requires. Generally, the list would likely include Employee Resource Groups, HR teams (including recruiting, leadership and development, compensation and benefits), Employer Branding, Communications, Corporate Responsibility, Legal and potentially others depending on your business structure.

10. Where your group is starting from

Before you begin meeting with the council, document your starting point, including the following:

- Has any work already been done related to the purpose of your group? If so, who has done this work? Talk to them; make sure you are not repeating work already done!

- Has any DEI-related data already been collected that would be helpful to review in advance?

- What other DEI groups or networks already exist in your organization, for example: working groups, advisory groups, Employee Resource Groups? Be sure to talk to them first to see how their purpose overlaps with yours.

- Are there any other structural barriers that would make the work of the group difficult or impossible?

The step of gathering this information prompts you to have conversations with important stakeholders and understand the context that is often unwritten. It also helps you set expectations by proactively having conversations about the council and its overlap with other groups.

Getting Started

Once you have the first draft of the governance document with the above elements, get feedback from a trusted sparring partner, and ideally, your champion.[1] As you consider who to invite to be a member of the council, actively strive for a group that is representative, diverse and reflects your organization geographically and across the areas of business. Make sure your invited members know what the commitment entails, so they are able to make an informed decision to participate. Send the governance document along as you invite people to join your group.

Once members have accepted, you are ready to schedule the inaugural meeting. Use the first meeting with the council to review the governance document, make any changes and get agreement to the governance from everyone before moving ahead. Make sure the council has the explicit ability to evolve the governance over time as needed.

---

[1] An executive level advocate who is willing to champion the DEI work and provide guidance and visibility. The role of the champion is explained in-depth in the next section: *How to create your organization's first DEI strategy.*

Going forward

As you move forward with the council, there are a few key things to keep in mind.

- Make sure each meeting has an agenda prepared and pre-read with the context of all the relevant topics that will be discussed. Send this out ahead of the meetings.

- Document the decisions and progress of your group going forward such as in a shared minutes document. Make sure all members of your group have access to this. Consider giving access to this documentation to important stakeholders to create transparency.

- Report your progress and success broadly. It's a good reminder that if you don't talk about what you are working on, people won't know. You could be doing a lot of great work *behind closed doors* but if your employees don't know it's happening, then to them, *it's NOT happening.* You've lost an opportunity to build trust and show progress.

- Be flexible to expand or change the structure if it's not working. If the council is too limited in scope or you are missing perspectives or insight from different parts of the business, grant the council the flexibility to evolve. If some members are unable to contribute the time and effort required, rotate membership as needed.

What does a successful DEI Council look like?

A successful council will help you set up your strategy and guide the implementation of your DEI work. It will help you solve ad hoc problems that arise or make broader decisions such as what partnerships to pursue. A successful council will also encourage its members to bring DEI back to their part of the organization and make it visible and relevant.

There is no one-size-fits-all approach. But it makes sense to start with something simple, relatively lean and flexible with the ability to evolve over time. Having your DEI council set up in advance will prime you for the next step: creating your DEI strategy.

How to create your organization's first DEI strategy

The task of creating a DEI strategy can seem impossible, especially if you are just one person taking on this task. To help you tackle this big undertaking, I've proposed a simple step-by-step process to get started. One thing to remember before you start: An effective DEI strategy will not be *short-term (6 months - 1 year)*. It should span several years to give you focus and create meaningful impact for the future. Much of the typical work contained within a DEI strategy takes months or years to put into place. I'd recommend a strategy that spans 3–5 years. There can be some flexibility to adjust it in the future, but it's important not to drastically change your focus too often.

What is a DEI Strategy and what can it do for you?

A DEI strategy will help you create focus in your work and translate your vision into practical goals. It will give you the chance to define the initiatives needed to achieve those goals. DEI is a unique topic compared to other strategic business topics. There are many, many different dimensions of diversity (race, religion, gender, disability, age, sexuality, etc.). It can be an easy pitfall to look at only one dimension of diversity and decide this is the *one thing* that deserves attention in your organization. This often happens with gender (for example: a strategy focused solely on women in leadership). I'd advise against this approach. This erases the experiences of others in your organization and gives the message that some groups are *more worthy* of attention than others. Instead, a better approach is a holistic strategy that doesn't prioritize individual identity groups.

A DEI strategy helps you focus your work. But what does this practically mean? There are so many things you could be working on at any given time, especially if your organization has never before focused on DEI as a strategic priority. Beginning this work can open the floodgates of ideas, projects and ambition. A good strategy will help protect you from spreading your work so thin that it lacks impact or becoming so overwhelmed that it's difficult to get anything off the ground. It also makes sure that you and your stakeholders know what your priorities are at any given time.

The following eight steps explain the process for creating a meaningful, holistic strategy that has buy-in from your organization. For context, most of these steps focus on the preparation and creation of buy-in that makes a strategy effective for an organization. This is a very important part; without this, you may end up with a very good strategy but no interest or dedication from the organization to implement it.

Step 1: Get the mandate

It can be tempting, as a member of an Employee Resource Group or just a passionate employee who cares about DEI, to begin the process of creating a company strategy on your own. But without the explicit *mandate* to do so, you may end up wasting your time. It's important to get the commitment from your organization before starting the work of creating a strategy. Talking with HR or your Corporate Responsibility team is a good place to start. This will also help you become aware of any work or research that has already been done that you could build upon.

Step 2: Find your champions

A good strategy is worthless if no one in the organization is willing to be accountable for it. Find someone from the leadership team (ideally an executive-level leader) dedicated to seeing meaningful change. Someone who is connected to HR is an obvious choice, but consider a champion outside of HR. This will further help you establish DEI as a *business priority.* If you are unable to find anyone in leadership willing to champion the DEI work, I would question whether the organization is genuinely willing to put the time and resources into making change happen. What should you look for when searching for a DEI champion in leadership?

- Someone very senior in the organization, ideally executive level
- Someone who will go into a room with their peers or people more senior than them and put their credit and visibility behind DEI work
- Someone who does not just *talk the talk* but also role models inclusive behaviors in their everyday lives
- Someone who can gather or allocate resources (budget or staff time) to support strategic DEI work
- Someone who is respected in your organization and would be willing to speak in support of the DEI work
- Someone well connected and willing to make meaningful introductions to stakeholders that are critical to success
- Someone willing to make time to provide guidance and advice
- Someone who understands and has a passion for DEI, recognizes their privilege, has already done the work to educate themselves and takes feedback humbly, without defensiveness

A DEI champion plays such a critical role in the success of DEI within an organization. They advise on the strategy and make sure it gets signed off on by the executive team. They make sure the DEI team is resourced in order to implement the strategy and help remove blockers that arise. I'd personally be hesitant to start any DEI work within an organization without a visible champion ready to support the work.

Step 3: Set up a council

Before setting up a strategy, it's important that you have identified a group that can support you in this task by advising and offering perspective from their area of the organization. The previous section details how to set up a DEI council. Involving them in creating the DEI

59

strategy will help ensure they are bought into the overall DEI approach and feel more comfortable championing it in their area of the organization.

Step 4: Understand your main challenges

Get to know your organization and document its unique challenges. Consider setting up focus groups to listen to employees' concerns or survey business leaders to understand their challenges. Minimally, before you start creating the strategy, you should understand the following:

- Has any DEI-related data already been collected that would be helpful to review?

- What DEI groups or networks already exist in your organization, for example: working groups, advisory groups, Employee or Resource Groups? Include them in the process of creating the strategy.

- Do you have any systemic issues of unfairness or discrimination that need to be addressed?

- Does your whistleblowing system[2] show any concerning patterns within parts of the business or geographically?

- Are there any other structural barriers that would make working on a DEI strategy difficult or impossible?

- Are there experts with skills in project management, strategy building, data analytics or other relevant experience that would be willing and able to contribute?

Have a frank conversation with your champion and DEI council to understand if the organization is willing to adopt an aligned strategy and provide resources (budget, work time) to materialize the work.

---

[2]A service that helps employees and others report malpractice and unlawful or unethical behavior within the workplace.

Step 5: Organize a workshop to create your strategy

Now it's time to create the strategy. There are many ways to do this. Sometimes people work with external experts[3] to develop the strategy, which is a great approach if you have the budget and commitment for that. But, if you have the above steps 1–4 in place and a good project management skillset to draw upon, it's possible to do this task internally. Here is a simple approach for a loosely structured workshop with your DEI council and a moderator to lead the session.

Get started by scheduling a 2-hour session and invite your DEI Council, DEI champion and key stakeholders (from relevant areas such as HR and Corporate Social Responsibility) that can provide valuable insight (max 8–10 people). This can be done virtually or in person. If remote, use a virtual whiteboard tool or collaborative document. Ask everyone to pre-read any relevant information gathered in step 4 before the workshop.

Agenda for the workshop

Reflection

At the beginning of the session, ask everyone to release their preconceived expectations on DEI and ideas for current initiatives and mentally start fresh. Ask them to close their eyes, and picture themselves five years in the future, with a cup of coffee in their hand, a clear mind and ask them to reflect on the achievements of the past five years. Ask everyone to imagine what (future) DEI achievements would make them proud as a member of the DEI council for your organization. Ask them to formulate these achievements into factual statements and write them down. Here are a few examples of such statements:

- We have a leadership team that is diverse and representative and can speak confidently and competently on DEI.

---

[3]Part 2: *How to hire a DEI consultant* explains what to expect from working with a DEI consultant and how to find the right one for you.

- All employees have the understanding and resources they need to contribute to an inclusive working environment.
- We have a working environment where everyone feels psychologically and physically safe.
- We support and empower a visible network of ERG communities and DEI advocates throughout the business.

Ask each participant to share their statements on a board and cluster them into similar achievements. These clusters will become the main strategy statements of your overall DEI strategy. For guidance, there's a comprehensive list of example strategy statements later in this section.

Separate these statements into two groups: internal and external. Internal refers to statements that relate to your employees and work culture. External meaning statements that refer to your customers, external partners, your industry or broader society.

Capture ideas for initiatives to achieve the strategy statements

Ask everyone to begin writing ideas for initiatives that would help the organization achieve these strategy statements. Ask each participant to share their initiative ideas on a board. Cluster them around each of the main strategy statements that they help to achieve. An initiative should be written so that it clearly supports achieving one of the main strategy statements. Note: identifying the right initiatives to support the strategy statements may need some additional support or external guidance. It's ok if you don't finish this step in the workshop.

Map stakeholders and barriers to success

Ask each participant to make a list of stakeholders that would need to be involved in putting those initiatives into place. Next, ask everyone to make a list of barriers to success, meaning any structural or organizational barrier that would make launching and achieving your DEI ambitions difficult. You'll need to try to address these before kicking off your work. (See: *How much does Diversity, Equity and Inclusion cost?* in Part 2 to better understand the commitments organizations must make to succeed in their DEI work.)

Final Reflections & expectation setting

Ask your council if they have anything else they want to add or make a note of. Ask them if they collectively agree with the strategy statements. Do a ROTI[4] exercise at the end of the session to see how effective the attendees found the session? Following the session, document all of the ideas and outcomes. The next step will be to prepare a draft of the strategy based on the input gathered in the session.

Step 6: Create the draft of the strategy document and align with stakeholders

Don't let too much time pass after the workshop. Create the first draft of the strategy within two weeks of the workshop. Here's how to create the first draft: Make a list of all of the strategy statements sorted by internal and external. If your strategy only focuses on internal work, set the external strategy statements aside for future reference. Create a maximum of 8 strategy statements. However, narrowing it down to just 5 or 6 statements will help you focus your work and balance ambition with realistic expectations.

Then list the ideas for initiatives that relate to each strategy statement. You may need to adjust this list of initiatives. I'd suggest a maximum of 5, but ideally only three initiatives per strategy statement. Make sure your initiatives are clear, contained and measurable. It's ok if not all initiatives are defined at this point. You can start with just one or two initiatives per strategy statement, expecting that more may be added in the future.

Share this first draft with your champion and DEI council and ask them to provide feedback. Make edits based on feedback, then

---

[4]ROTI: *Return on Time Invested*, an exercise to ask participants to reflect on how useful the session was, if it met their expectations and could it be improved in some way.

expand the review process to other stakeholders such as those you listed during the workshop or your Employee Resource Groups. You may consider having a few feedback sessions to capture this insight efficiently.

Finally, ask your DEI council and champion to officially sign off on the strategy. Next, work with your champion to present to your organization's executive team so they can approve the strategy. This may be the most critical role of your champion: to help get this senior-level endorsement. Their agreement is critical because it signals to your stakeholders that the leaders are on board and committed to the strategy. Ideally, at this same stage, you will estimate the budget and resources needed to accomplish the strategy and request this from the relevant budget holder.[5] Keep in mind, resourcing of budget or hiring may take several months to materialize, which would delay your ability to begin the work.

Step 7: Create a roadmap with accountable owners

From your list of initiatives, identify which can be completed first and use this to create a roadmap. It will likely make sense to only create a roadmap for the first year of initiatives. Make sure each initiative in the roadmap has a metric to track its success and an accountable owner within your organization. Try to be realistic about what can reasonably be accomplished in your first year. Some initiatives take many months to achieve. It's better to be conservative in your ambitions in your first year.

Step 8: Start doing the work and track your progress

Schedule a kickoff with your stakeholders and present the roadmap of planned work. If you have multiple owners of the initiatives, make sure they are all aware of their relevant initiatives. Schedule a regular check-in (monthly) with the owners of the initiatives so they can report back on their progress and share any blockers or challenges they face.

---

[5]The section *How much does Diversity, Equity and Inclusion cost?* in Part 2 includes an explanation of how to estimate a budget based on your strategy.

A few tips to keep in mind as you create the first strategy:

- Including the preparation time and alignment, developing a strategy takes a substantial amount of time, likely at least three months. Do not jump into work on initiatives until you have an aligned strategy. This helps maintain focus on creating the strategy and avoid wasting effort on initiatives that may get scrapped.

- A strategy that focuses on just one dimension of diversity (for example, gender) will quickly become too limited in scope to adequately address DEI. A holistic strategy has a much better chance of properly addressing the needs of your organization.[6]

- Employee Resource Groups have first-hand knowledge of your organization's biggest challenges. Engage them in the review of the strategy and incorporate their suggestions. This helps you learn from their experiences and also creates more buy-in on the grassroots, employee level.

- Be realistic in scope and timing. A lot of this work takes a substantial amount of time to do correctly. It can be tempting to make a very ambitious strategy that promises the moon then quickly fails to deliver. This can be demoralizing for you as well as your stakeholders.

- You will need data to help you track your success and understand if you are achieving your goals. You may need to identify partners within HR or another relevant area that can contribute their expertise to develop and track relevant metrics for your strategy. (The next section *How to measure the impact of your work?* discusses this.)

---

[6]It is a common pattern for organizations to initially launch a strategy that only focuses on a few dimensions of diversity (gender, internationality, for example) and then a year or so later (typically after getting feedback from their employees), develop a new strategy with a holistic approach. Avoid this common mistake and start with a holistic strategy from the beginning.

For inspiration, here are some example strategy statements for both internal and external focused strategies.

Internal statements:

- "All of our employees and prospective applicants experience equitable and unbiased hiring and promotion processes."
- "Everyone in the organization, and especially leaders, contribute to inclusion by understanding and delivering on their individual responsibility to create an inclusive and psychologically safe working environment."
- "Our Employee Resource Groups are visible, supported and empowered to achieve their own goals, support their communities and be a resource to the organization by advising on business decisions."
- "Our leadership team is diverse and representative of the greater customer base and industry."

External statements:

- "Our product and services have been designed to serve a diverse audience, with input from expert communities to create inclusive experiences."
- "We support the broader ecosystem of our industry by providing mentoring and education to actively create equitable opportunities and inclusion in the industry."
- "We take an active stance on DEI in society by communicating our goals within the industry, sharing thought leadership and setting a high bar for others to follow."

There is no perfect one-size-fits-all approach, but this set of steps can be a relatively lean and flexible way to create a first DEI strategy. This approach is especially useful if you are creating your organization's first ever strategy and you are driving this as the sole responsible employee working on DEI. Ideally, this method helps create a strategy that has buy-in across the organization (thanks to your DEI champion, council and stakeholders) and is ambitious but manageable over time with measurable initiatives to achieve.

And one final note: DEI work can feel very incremental and slow while actually doing the work, so it's essential to recognize the progress you have made over time to stay motivated. In the next section we'll explore how to measure the impact your work has.

How to measure the impact of your work

If you are unable to track the progress of your DEI Work, you will not know if the work is actually having an impact and if you are achieving the overall goals of your strategy. This section explores how to develop practical and meaningful metrics to measure and communicate the impact of your work.

There are two types of metrics: input and output. *Input* refers to metrics relating to the intervention or changes you are making, and *output* refers to the results of the interventions. In general, if you want to assess impact, it's best to measure output metrics, but in some situations input metrics also make sense. To make this distinction more concrete, here's an example: if you have a strategic goal to increase the inclusion of employees in your organization, an input metric would measure something that increases inclusion (such as membership in Employee Resource Groups). And the output measure would be whether the employees *feel* a greater sense of inclusion (likely measured with an employee survey). Output metrics make sure you are having the intended impact. In this example, it may be that you have a lot of employees involved in ERGs, but if that doesn't translate into an increase in inclusion, the initiative is not actually contributing to that specific strategic goal.

Here are a series of considerations to help you in developing meaningful and realistic metrics.

Measurability: Keep in mind that some of the impacts of DEI work are difficult to measure or associate directly with specific initiatives.

Changing an organization's culture happens through many, many small actions and behaviors, and it's not always easy to directly connect the dots.

It's also tempting to develop many metrics, but that also creates a lot of overhead and even wasted effort if you do not measure the right things. Create only a limited number of meaningful metrics. Start with 3 to 5 that are most representative of the impact you wish to have based on your strategy. And, of course, make sure they are possible to track. Spending too much time developing and monitoring metrics detracts from the time you have to drive DEI work. The possibility of measuring some metrics will depend on the maturity of your HR data systems or whether you have support from data-savvy stakeholders in HR or other parts of your organization.

Stakeholder expectations: Often, stakeholders want to see a dashboard with a live stream of all possible metrics. This would be nice, but it takes a lot of time to maintain and manage, especially if data feeds (for example, from surveys or hiring) are not already available. When you are just getting started, a quarterly email with a short list of key metrics is a more realistic approach.

Surveys: Many common DEI metrics rely on a regular internal survey on inclusion and identity. In Part 5, the section *Creating an employee inclusion and identity survey* explores how to set this up. A well-crafted survey is a great tool to understand your organization's baseline and track progress over time. But it requires care and thought to put in place in a trustworthy and meaningful way.

Baselines: To show progress, it's important to know where you are *starting from* Before you can set targets or goals, you need to measure your baseline, likely using a survey as mentioned above. Once that is done, you can then set the target you would like to achieve. For example, if you want to increase inclusion in your organization, you need to first understand the baseline experiences of inclusion across your organization before you can decide what increase is possible. It doesn't make sense to set a target if you don't know where you are starting from.

With all that in mind, let's get to the practical examples. Here is a list of strategy statements, the related DEI initiative for each and a suggestion for a meaningful metric. (By the way, this may serve as inspiration for the strategy setting task in the previous section!)

Strategy Statement: "All leaders in the organization actively participate in DEI skill-building to increase their understanding and role modeling."

Initiative: Develop and deploy a skill-building curriculum for leaders which includes inclusive leadership training and supports senior leaders to lead difficult conversations about DEI.

Metric: An input metric would be the number of leaders that have participated in the training program. But a more meaningful output metric would measure the impact of the training. This could be measured with a survey among the leaders (sent before and after the training) with a question such as "How confident do you feel to deliver on your responsibility to role model inclusive behavior?" Alternatively, another output metric could look at whether the training program is having an impact in teams throughout the organization. A global inclusion survey could ask whether "My Team's manager demonstrates a visible commitment to diversity and inclusion."

Strategy Statement: "All of our prospective applicants and employees experience equitable and unbiased hiring and promotion processes."

Initiative: Develop a DEI Recruiting Checklist for use in hiring to reach a diverse shortlist of candidates and make fair and unbiased decisions. Create accountability for the use of the checklist for everyone involved in hiring and promotions.

Metric: The percentage of open positions where the hiring checklist is actively used is a relevant input metric. A meaningful output metric would measure the impact of the use of the checklist, for example, the diversity of new hires or the results of a survey sent to applicants on their perception of the fairness of the process.

Strategy Statement: "Everyone in the organization contributes to inclusion by understanding and delivering on their individual responsibility to create an inclusive and safe working environment."

Initiative: Create ownership of DEI throughout the organization by empowering and upskilling DEI Advocates as multipliers in their region and business area and providing them resources and training to do so.

Metric: The number of advocates in your organization would be the input metric. Alternatively, the percentage of office locations or business areas in your organization that is represented by advocates could serve as an input metric. An output metric could be measured through the results of a survey to see if employees feel that DEI is embedded in their area and driven locally in a relevant way.

Strategy Statement: "Our Employee Resource Groups are visible, supported and empowered to achieve their own goals and support their communities."

Initiative: Develop a resource toolkit that provides guidance on governance and problem-solving for common challenges to support ERGs to launch and organize effectively.

Metrics: The number of resources in the toolkit would be the input metric. An output metric would measure the impact that those resources have for the ERGs. This could be measured by surveying the ERG leaders on whether the resources improve their organizing. Alternatively, the output metric could measure the maturity level of ERGs, for example, whether they each have a strategy in place and a leadership team with clear roles defined.

A final note: Keep in mind, the metrics are only as good as the data feeding in. This underscores the point that it's better to measure fewer meaningful, representative and accurate metrics than tracking everything that could possibly be measured. Importantly, give yourself permission to interrogate your metrics. After the first year, check-in and ask: are these metrics measuring the impact we wish to have with our strategy? Are they meaningful to our stakeholders? If they are no longer meaningful or not representative of the intended impact of your work, consider taking a different approach.

How and what to communicate about DEI

You may be doing fantastic work on DEI, but no one will know it's happening if you don't communicate it. Employees passionate about DEI want to know what the organization is doing and how they can contribute. So, let's explore best practices for communicating internally about DEI.

Making resources and information about your strategy accessible and up to date is very helpful to your DEI efforts. But how? Most organizations have an internal communication platform for sharing information with employees (one that is not accessible by an external audience). This is often called an intranet and it is the most important portal to use in your communication. As you plan what content to share on the DEI page on the intranet, think about what would be most helpful to your employees. Think about what type of questions you get regularly, and make sure to cover those on your page. The following list has the critical information to include.

Core content

- *What does DEI mean in your organization?* Include definitions you use, statements made by leadership or videos defining your vision.
- *Who is involved in DEI?* Highlight the key contacts, including the DEI team, your champion(s) and members of the DEI council.

- *Strategy and Active Initiatives:* Include a summary of your strategy and the active initiatives you are driving. Include the current status and point of contact for each initiative.

Resources & Links

- *Essential Reading:* Include blogs or articles that explain core DEI concepts such as allyship, equity, intersectionality, microaggressions and privilege.
- *Training:* Include links to available training on topics such as unconscious bias, anti-harassment, anti-racism, inclusive language and inclusive behavior. If you do not have training content created internally, you can link to high-quality external training videos available online.
- *Links to essential resources:* Include additional links to relevant resources or processes such as your Speak Up (whistleblowing) system, salary transparency reporting, inclusive language guidelines and the employee Code of Conduct.

Employee Resource Groups

Include information that helps employees understand, find and start Employee Resource Groups.

- *Introducing the ERG Program:* Explain the program, what type of groups are in scope and what support is offered.
- *How to start your ERG?* Share a step-by-step guide to support employees in starting their own ERG and who can support them in doing so.
- *A list of your ERGs:* Include links to all existing ERGs and the contact information of their leadership teams.
- *Resources for ERGs:* Include guides on strategy setting communicating, organizing events and collaborating with stakeholders.

Blog Posts

In addition to static content on your page, create a schedule of topical posts to publish on an ongoing basis. These blogs can announce important strategic milestones you've achieved or just present opportunities to learn about topics related to DEI. For inspiration, consult international calendars of relevant advocacy dates (such as Black History Month, Autism Awareness Month, Trans Visibility Day). Create blogs that highlight and acknowledge these. Invite your Employee Resource Groups to contribute to this content to make sure it is authentic and centers their voices. You can also create blogs that recap events, list books to read or highlights podcasts, videos or webinar recordings. These topical blogs should be short, educational content that keep employees engaged in your DEI work.

Launching your DEI page

Launching your page for the first time can require a lot of preparation. But it's also a significant milestone. Make sure you have all (or at least most) of your core content prepared before launch. Pre-publish a few blog posts to show some activity on your page. Feature your ERGs and give them a substantial amount of visibility on the page.

For DEI to be perceived as a strategic, company-wide topic, it's important that your work is not seen as an isolated topic (for example, only relevant to ERGs and HR). One way to avoid this is to ask the leadership team to showcase and communicate the work of the DEI team. This helps embed your work into your company culture and position it as an essential and strategic business topic. Ask your DEI champion(s) or other members of the leadership team to share the content within their networks to give it more visibility. If you have weekly, company-wide newsletters or messages sent out internally, make sure your page is highlighted there.

Create ongoing engagement with your content

As you plan new blog posts, invite your leadership team to get involved. They can post blogs directly from their account to give them more visibility or simply comment on or share existing posts. Speaking of visibility, as new ERGs launch, ask your leadership team to show support for the new groups by commenting and endorsing them.

Keep your content fresh and relevant

Make sure your content is fresh, up to date and offers many ways for employees to engage. Here are some tips to make sure the content is current and relevant:

- Provide regular updates on your main initiatives and progress towards your strategy with the metrics you are tracking.
- Make sure people know how to get involved with existing ERGs or how to start their own.
- Follow a blog posting schedule to develop regular, topical content for your page (1–2 times per month). Make sure all blogs have an action for further engagement, including a book to read, a movie to watch or a training session to take.
- Share and highlight blogs, events and announcements of your ERGs to give them visibility and recognition.
- Revisit your core content (definitions, essential reading and key contacts) twice per year to ensure it is still relevant. If not, update it.
- Offer many ways for employees to engage with DEI in a self-directed way, including tips for launching a reading club within their team or curriculums for self-guided learning.

Authenticity and tone

Especially for DEI communication, the content should feel authentic. But even if your intention is authenticity, your communication may not always come off that way. This is especially true if your communication has a more formal or corporate tone.[7] The reality is that people want to hear honesty from your organization, not sugarcoating, doublespeak or empty promises. It's pretty powerful to admit to a failure or that something within your organization needs improvement followed by an honest commitment to investing in a solution and plans to provide regular updates. If you are worried that your content does not have the right tone of authenticity, ask for feedback from your employees, DEI Council or external communication experts. Then, take that feedback to heart and use it to improve your messaging.

Be sure to frequently give the stage to your Employee Resource Groups whenever you can. Invite them to contribute content or co-author with you. Especially during key dates such as International Women's Day or Black History Month, welcome your ERGs to craft meaningful content on behalf of their communities. This gives authenticity to the content and highlights the experiences and perspectives of your ERGs.

Final thoughts on communication

Communicating frequently and transparently is the best way to keep your audience updated and engaged in your work. It's better to over-inform than under-inform. If you are working on great DEI initiatives but no one knows about them, then employees in your organization will assume no work is being done. Don't let that happen!

And a final note about inclusive language: Inclusive language is uniquely relevant for your DEI communication. In Part 5: *Deep Dive: Creating Inclusion in the Workplace* and in the appendix: *Inclusive Language Guide*, we discuss the core concepts of inclusive language.

---

[7]The book *On Writing Well* by William Zinsser has been a big inspiration to me and many others on the topic of writing and communicating with clarity and impact.

PART 4:
EVERYTHING ABOUT EMPLOYEE RESOURCE GROUPS

Employee Resource Groups are critical stakeholders for creating your first DEI strategy and they deserve visibility in your communication. Now it's time we really dive into ERGs. This part of the book is all about Employee Resource Groups. Setting up an Employee Resource Group program that offers support, engagement and empowerment to the communities in your organization is one of the most fundamental steps towards building an inclusive working environment. Let's explore the purpose of ERGs, how to help them set up and how to recognize their work.

Understanding Employee Resource Groups

Employee Resource Groups (or ERGs) are employee identity or experience-based groups. ERGs are sometimes known as Affinity Groups or Diversity Groups.[1] They are employee-led[2] and focused on building community, providing support and contributing to personal and professional development in the work environment. Many large companies have ERG programs including Uber, Salesforce, Amazon, Google and Siemens.[3]

What is the purpose of an ERG program?

- It provides the organizational structure to existing or prospective employee groups by putting a framework in place for launching new ERGs and establishing governance.

- It creates an open forum for employees who share a common identity to meet and support one another in building their community and sense of belonging.

- It supports these groups by offering them financial support, organizational support and access to decision-makers.

- It facilitates a clear line of communication from ERGs to leadership to voice concerns and solve problems and it seeks to advance a respectful and inclusive company culture.

---

[1] Some organizations use the term *Business Resource Groups*. In some cases, BRGs function the same as ERGs, in other cases, they are more focused on advising and guiding the business on topics relevant to the BRG's community.

[2] ERGs are founded voluntarily in a self-led, grassroots manner, not designed or dictated top-down by leadership.

[3] Smaller organizations (for example: fewer than 100 employees) may not have enough employees to organize an ERG based on a given identity. Instead, an approach may be to set up a general Diversity ERG to begin to build community and a collective voice on inclusion topics despite not having a critical mass for individual community groups.

What value do ERGs bring to your organization?

ERGs bring value to your organization and its employees in several ways. They build a sense of community and belonging for employees by connecting people socially and professionally. Second, they empower employees by giving each group a collective voice to speak with decision-makers and leadership. ERGs often support professional development by creating formal and informal leadership opportunities and creating visibility for employees. ERGs also provide a resource for leadership and decision-makers regarding staff issues, needs and policies. ERGs offer their expertise and experiences to improve equity within their organization. They can also be an asset in business decisions to make better, more inclusive products and services. Lastly, ERGs support retention because employees are likely to stay with the company longer if they are part of a strong community within the company and feel a sense of belonging.

Which ERGs typically form?

ERGs develop based on shared identities or experiences. Below is a list of ERGs that typically form. This is an incomplete list; each organization defines the scope of their ERG program in their own way and may include other special-interest or community groups.

- Cultural, racial and ethnic identities
- People with disabilities or neurodiversity
- Gender-based groups, including women, transgender or nonbinary gender identities
- Religion or faith-based communities
- Sexual orientation communities
- Age or generational communities
- Parents including groups for single parents and caregivers

ERGs typically form from groups that are marginalized or underrepresented.

Why is community important in a working environment?

Psychological safety and a sense of belonging are essential to give employees the space and security to be themselves at work. Specifically for employees working in teams, this increases collaboration and effectiveness. When employees are members of a strong network or community, it helps create this sense of belonging. In order to truly empower and support ERGs, they need to have the autonomy to define the scope of their group, membership eligibility and most importantly, what success means for them.

Supporting & empowering Employee Resource Groups

Establishing an ERG program is one way for an organization to work towards an inclusive company culture. But simply launching a program is not enough to empower and support ERGs. A successful Employee Resource Group program needs to support groups to form, be visible and create the impact they wish to have. The governance of the ERG program should include a collection of resources to help them be as successful and impactful as possible. Here's a list of guides to create to support ERGs:

- How to launch a new Employee Resource Group (including a template of an ERG Charter document and any other application information necessary to launch)
- How to create a strategy for an ERG
- How to create a community page for an ERG on your organization's intranet
- How to host events (virtual and in-person)
- Budget request process and budget tracking template
- How to collaborate with the organization on a project

There are some fantastic free, open-source ERG playbooks and toolkits available online which can support you in setting up these documents.[4]

To further help ERGs set their goals, provide support to help the ERG set their strategy and measure their success. This could include offering a strategy workshop, templates to develop and define their project roadmap and support setting and tracking their goals.

What is a sponsor, and how can they support an ERG?

Sponsorship[5] is an integral part of a successful ERG program. Sponsorship from the executive team (or other senior leaders) shows that the organization stands behind the ERGs and offers their support, which typically includes guidance, mentoring, visibility and networking to support their success. A sponsor will make the success of the ERG a priority and their personal responsibility without taking ownership or taking away autonomy of the group. Specifically, a sponsor provides:

- **Visibility** to raise awareness of the ERG and their needs by contributing to ERG events, communicating about the ERG and making connections to relevant people and organizations.

- **Strategic guidance** to align the goals of the ERG with the organization's business strategy by supporting the ERG to define their bold vision of what can be accomplished.

- **Coaching & mentorship** to guide the ERG leadership team to ensure strategic thinking and by providing meaningful leadership coaching and support, especially as obstacles arise.

---

[4]Examples: *https://coda.io/@rachelc/codas-employee-resource-group-playbook/starting-an-erg-2*

[5]Podcast: *Executive Sponsors Fuel High-Performing ERGs* by Jennifer Brown Consulting, 2018. *https://open.spotify.com/episode/6vQeRaup1VvPT/5giJSnDm*

What qualities make a good ERG sponsor?

- Someone who is respected and willing to go into a room with their peers to advocate on behalf of the ERG, meaning someone willing to put their credit and visibility behind the ERG

- Someone who has some ability to allocate resources to back an important ERG project

- Someone well connected and willing to make meaningful introductions to stakeholders who are crucial to the success of strategic ERG projects

- Someone willing to make time, approximately 2-4 hours per month, to offer mentorship, guidance and advice to the ERG (typically through a regular meeting or ad hoc as needed).

- Someone who has a sufficient understanding of DEI, has already done the work to educate themselves and takes feedback humbly, without defensiveness.

Some ERGs find it very important to identify a sponsor that is a member of their own community, whereas others don't find this necessary. It's important for the ERG to find a sponsor that is right for them develop a good working relationship. A note on the seniority of sponsors: sponsors do not necessarily need to be at the top seniority level. In fact, I've found that having a passionate leader at a less senior level can be more impactful than a very senior leader who is less engaged and committed. In choosing a sponsor, ERGs need to find someone who is willing to put their own privilege and reputation on the line for the ERG and is personally committed to the group's success.

Recognizing & rewarding Employee Resource Groups

Many employees actively involved in Employee Resource Groups find the experience personally and professionally rewarding. It gives them an additional sense of purpose in the workplace and makes them an active part of the company's DEI efforts. But just because an employee finds this work personally rewarding does not mean the company shouldn't recognize it as well.

Why should companies reward ERG work?

ERGs bring value to your organization in many ways. Organizations often broadcast the work of ERGs in press releases to showcase how diverse and inclusive they are. ERGs are even featured in branding campaigns to attract new employees. Organizations get a lot of value from ERGs. So why shouldn't this work be officially recognized and rewarded? Organizations have all sorts of creative arrangements to incentivize and reward different types of work outside of core job responsibilities (such as being part of hiring committees, writing content for external blogs and speaking at conferences). Work in ERGs is absolutely on par with these efforts because it also improves the organization's culture and helps market the organization as an attractive place to work.

The difficulty is that many organizations interpret the work of ERG organizers as "passion project" work. They see ERG organizers as willing to give their free time because it's a personal interest topic. But sadly, that mindset underestimates and undervalues this work. When this work is interpreted as "free time" work, it perpetuates the assumption that the organization does not benefit from it in a way that deserves compensation or recognition.

ERG work can indeed be fun but it's also a massive amount of *work*. To frame it correctly, I'd suggest not to call this "volunteer" work; instead, I'd put it in a context that represents the value it brings: "Cultural Work." This is work that directly benefits the organization's culture. In general, this boils down to an organization recognizing and valuing this work as strategically beneficial to employees and the organization. And in doing so, validating it. Let's explore all the ways your organization can recognize and reward ERG organizers.

Set ERGs up for success

One of the most important things an organization can do to support and acknowledge the work of ERG organizers is to set them up for success. In practice, this means putting processes and structures in place that help ERGs be successful and visible. This includes developing a governance structure for how ERGs are formed, organized and sponsored. It also means setting clear boundaries about what ERGs can be expected to drive and what they should not be expected to drive. This is critical to make sure ERGs don't become the go-to team to solve all of an organization's DEI challenges. It's also essential to make sure they don't become owners of critical HR processes or legal processes. Additionally, it's important to provide ERGs with resources and guidance to support them, including documentation on how to set their own strategy, organize events, collaborate with the organization and find out who their key contacts are. And most critical for the success of ERGs: offer them each a budget. This doesn't need to be massive. But providing funding to the ERGs shows that your organization values and trusts their work and gives them the opportunity to work on more ambitious projects.

Recognize ERG work in formal structures

Organizations typically have processes in place to recognize and evaluate their employees. During performance review periods, employees have the opportunity to discuss and acknowledge their success at work, perhaps making the case for a promotion or a raise. Contributions to an ERG should absolutely fall within that scope. This acknowledgment communicates top-down that work within an ERG is relevant in these conversations and deserving of recognition. Communication that ERG work is in scope for these discussions needs to come top-down otherwise managers are often unsure of how to interpret this work. Speaking of managers, they will also need guidance on how to support their employees involved in ERG organizing. Offering them explicit guidance and FAQs gives them the tools to be supportive allies.

If employees set yearly objectives or targets that are rewarded by bonuses, clearly communicate that ERG work fits within that context. To make this more tangible, offer example objectives or targets that relate to ERG work. And lastly, as employees move internally (by applying for a promotion or another internal role), it should be clear that their work with an ERG is recognized as relevant professional growth. The skills that ERG organizers build (communication, project management, strategy development and leadership) are absolutely applicable to career growth and should be recognized as such.

Pay ERG organizers for the work they do

The most straightforward way to reward ERG organizing is of course to pay for it.[6] It's easiest to utilize an existing target-based or discretionary bonus program. If a bonus is not open for consideration, consider offering an additional professional development stipend to attend conferences or training programs.

ERG organizing time as work time

Organizations typically have programs to acknowledge activities that are not "strictly" business work as part of an employee's paid time. This includes professional development time (to learn new skills) or research time (to explore innovative projects). Those examples are clearly recognized as work. So why does ERG work often get relegated to an employee's "free time"? I would theorize (without evidence) that it is perhaps because it's usually women and people from marginalized

---

[6]Companies that have introduced bonuses for ERG organizers:

Uber: *https://medium.com/@l.research.co/women-leading-the-underground-movement-to-support-caregivers-at-work-a35dca0f4628*

LinkedIn: *https://www.linkedin.com/business/talent/blog/talent-acquisition/simple-way-companies-can-invest-in-diversity-inclusion*

Twitter: *https://blog.twitter.com/en_us/topics/company/2020/inclusion-and-diversity-report-blacklivesmatter-september-2020*

groups doing this ERG work and it's easier for decision-makers to perceive their work as "free."

In the same vein as "Research Time" or "Professional Development Time," organizations can simply offer a percentage of time for ERG work for organizers. I'd suggest 5-10 percent allocated work time for the organizers of ERGs (approximately 2-4 hours per week). Offering allocated work time is a clear message to employees that ERG work *is work* and the organization perceives it that way.

Create opportunities for ERG organizers

Another type of reward is to offer ERG organizers access to unique opportunities for growth, development and networking. This can be done by setting up a mentorship program for ERG organizers, creating networking opportunities to connect with other organizers internally and externally or by offering opportunities to participate in special programs or conferences to help build their leadership skills.

Give Visibility to ERG Organizers

Offering visibility to ERGs is an important way their work can be acknowledged. This can be done by offering professional branding to design ERG logos, inviting ERG organizers to meet with the executive team and present their accomplishments, host a video series of interviews or discussions between the ERGs and the CEO, feature blog posts and events from the ERGs in weekly newsletters and encourage ERG members to include their ERG logo in their email signatures. All of these ideas are quite simple, but they go a long way to validate, showcase and acknowledge the work of ERGs.

Final thoughts on Recognizing ERG Work

ERGs are an asset to your organization and DEI efforts by voicing concerns of employees, providing relevant feedback and guidance and increasing inclusion. Giving ERGs the tools, structure and support they need helps make sure the relationship between the organization and the ERGs is collaborative and fruitful. It requires a mindset shift to recognize the work of ERGs, not as a fluffy community volunteer project but as valuable work that contributes to the health of the organization.

Building bridges and managing expectations

Many of the people I know working in DEI started their professional journey by becoming involved with an ERG in the workplace or through community activist work. That engagement led them to opportunities to work in DEI in a professional capacity. But the work that happens within ERG or activist spaces tends to be quite different than the painstakingly slow change management and strategic DEI work that happens in an organizational setting. This mindset shift can be personally challenging to transcend. It also requires a different set of skills for success (we covered this in Part 2: *What skills are most useful for a DEI role?*). On top of that, there are some very real conflicts that emerge when we are working in DEI while also trying to empower ERGs.

In supporting ERGs and paving the way for their successful collaboration with stakeholders in Human Resources or other parts of your organization, there is often some degree of misaligned expectations. This sometimes stems from a disconnect between what ERGs want to achieve and what an organization is willing to do. Sometimes this is a result of a conflict between what ERGs think their role is and what the organization thinks their role is. Personally, I've found these conflicts difficult to navigate. ERGs are such important stakeholders in the success of our collective DEI work and their inclusion and validation are essential in a diverse workplace. Their agenda and strategic goals are valid and worthwhile. I *want* them to succeed in achieving those goals. But as DEI professionals, we are often somehow caught in the middle between ERGs and their stakeholders who are critical to their success. We try to encourage a mutual understanding. I know this can be especially challenging for my colleagues who are both working full-time in DEI and also active members of ERGs.

I think this conflict boils down to the fact that DEI professionals are often working within HR and they are trying to represent the needs of HR and the organization as well as the needs of the employees. Sometimes these are not the same. To speak generally, often HR is not keen to provide what employees need or want.

When I've reached an impasse while supporting ERGs to collaborate with their stakeholders, I've managed this by being candid and authentic. I try to explain to the ERGs who their relevant stakeholders are and what *their* motivations are. I offer my view on what is the best course of action to achieve what the ERGs want, leveraging my understanding of the innerworkings of corporate politics. Sometimes I advise ERGs to engage their sponsor to utilize their support and influence to push their agenda. Sometimes I advise them to focus on short-term achievable goals in service of a long-term strategy.

On the stakeholder side, our role as DEI professionals is often to explain the value ERGs bring to the organization, what their motivations are and encourage them to support ERG initiatives. Sometimes we function in a spokesperson role, sometimes as a bridge-builder and sometimes as a mediator. This can be a fine line to walk.

So, how can we, as DEI professionals, build the bridge between ERG organizers and stakeholders who are critical to their success? Here are eleven steps:

1. To stakeholders and decision-makers: over-communicate the value ERGs bring to your organization and what role they play. If this is documented in an ERG strategy that is aligned top-down, even better. It's great to have a resource you can point to that clearly states the role and function of ERGs in your organization.

2. Proactively share the organizational structure of ERGs (including the roles of sponsors, organizers and members) so stakeholders understand how they are set up and can build trusting relationships with the organizers of the ERGs.

3. Recognize and reward the work of ERG organizers in official channels. This elevates the work to a professional level and goes far to validate it within the workplace.

4. Help ERGs identify their spokesperson. This helps their stakeholders understand who to coordinate with and avoids multiple threads of communication. Similarly, develop a contact list of relevant partners and stakeholders of ERGs to make their outreach more direct and efficient.

5. Develop a guide on how ERGs collaborate with HR and the rest of your organization. Include the process for how ERGs may propose a project or request support. Take the time to align this process with HR and business leaders.

6. Explain to ERGs what they can expect from leaders in your organization. The reality is, most leaders are not natural, skilled speakers on complex DEI topics such as allyship, intersectionality or privilege.[7] Most will need a substantial amount of upskilling when asked to speak on short notice on one of those topics. Being transparent about this helps set expectations and create empathy.

7. Give ERGs the tools to develop their own strategy including what they want to accomplish and by when. Encourage them to publish this internally. Ideally, this is somewhat aligned with your broader DEI strategy and can work in tandem.

8. Explain to ERGs who the decision-makers are for the project they want to drive. They may think you, in your DEI role, are the person deciding on all DEI-related matters. But we know, in practice, that there are many other stakeholders who own the processes of interest to ERGs (such as hiring, compensation,

---

[7]To illustrate this: I recently had a conversation with a friend working in DEI. They told me "If only I could sit down with the CEO and ask him what his vision is for disability inclusion, then we could really get started working on this. I told them, "Your CEO doesn't have a vision on disability inclusion. He's likely never spent any time thinking about it. That's why they hired you, to tell him what his vision is." This assumption that CEOs naturally have all the answers and can speak with no prep on any topic is very common, and very wrong.

promotions, culture, anti-discrimination reporting and many more). Giving them visibility on the decision-makers helps them know where to invest their time to build those relationships and influence decisions.

9. Coach ERGs on where their energy is best spent. If there are topics that you know will probably be a dead-end for an ERG to drive, be open and transparent about this. The ERG may still decide to continue their advocacy on these topics, or they may decide to focus their effort elsewhere, in a more fruitful direction.

10. Advise ERGs on the best way to leverage their relationships with stakeholders and leaders to move their strategy forward. This includes their sponsor as well as other senior leaders that have influence within the organization.

11. Importantly, explain *your* role as a DEI professional who is functioning as a connector and bridge-builder in these conversations. Oftentimes, we are in a relatively neutral position, doing our best to help everyone collaborate better. Make that position transparent and visible.

Another common frustration I hear from ERGs is they do not see the impact of our DEI work. They perceive it as not happening fast enough or not directly supporting their communities. What is the root cause of this frustration? Likely, one of the following:

- ERGs may not understand that impactful DEI work takes a lot of time, and organizations are big, complex machines that move slowly and break often. Any quick solution will lack substance and long-term impact.

- There is impactful work happening but it's not visible to ERGs either because they don't have a seat at the decision making table or because the work is not being communicated broadly in internal channels.

- ERGs have a specific expectation of what impact relevant to their community they would like to see, and they don't see it because it's not happening.

These are each separate challenges with unique solutions. The first one can be addressed by being very transparent about all the dependencies that affect our work and that impactful DEI initiatives in an organizational setting take a lot of time to do correctly. The second one can be addressed through increased communication and inviting representatives of your ERGs to be involved in the DEI Council or decision making bodies. The last one is more complicated. Understandably, ERGs are keen to see impactful work that is relevant to their communities. Their expectation of what they'd like to see happen does not always match the planned work in your DEI strategy. Inviting ERGs to be involved in the creation of the DEI strategy is one way to get their input early on and make sure they have buy-in from the beginning. How you create your strategy also plays a part here. Prioritize developing a strategy that is holistic instead of focusing on just one or two identifies. In your communication, make sure you highlight the importance of an intersectional approach to DEI.

And finally, what happens when there is a substantial conflict between your ERGs and your organization? What if your ERGs organize a walk-out in protest of a decision made by leadership or a transphobic stand-up comedy special you broadcasted? I honestly have a lot of empathy for DEI professionals in these situations. Likely, they are not the ones who made these business decisions, but they have to do a substantial amount of work to "clean up the mess." So, what is the role of the DEI professional in these situations? Is it damage control or walking out alongside the ERG? Or do they function as a mediator? There's no perfect answer here and every situation is a bit different. If you find yourself in this situation, I think it's worth figuring out what your organization and its leaders expect you to do. Then you must decide whether this is something that matches your values and you are comfortable doing. Are you willing to play the role they want you to play?

Do you maintain your integrity? And then ask your organization: are business leaders willing to revisit the decision making process to prevent a similar situation in the future? Do they recognize the situation as a failure that caused harm or do they stand by their decision and invite offended employees to leave the company? In situations like these, I often feel the most conflicted about doing DEI work in a for-profit corporate setting.

To summarize, a common theme in this bridge-building work is transparency, authenticity and over-communicating. But in the end, not every collaboration will be a win all around. I often see ourselves (DEI professionals) as the brokers of compromise between ERGs and their stakeholders, trying to come to a mutual understanding and find a willingness to collaborate across all sides. In the end, this is not always satisfying for everyone involved, despite requiring a lot of effort on our part. The reality is that sometimes it can be immensely disappointing and make us feel like we are shortchanging our own communities. But at other times, it can be hugely empowering to support an ERG to launch and flourish, becoming a critical safe space for their community. It's a mixed bag.

PART 5:
DEEP DIVE: IMPACTFUL DEI INITIATIVES

The first part of the book was all about understanding DEI in the workplace and setting for success by putting key pieces in place like a strategy and governance to guide your DEI work. Now let's talk about *the actual work* of activating the strategy. This chapter has examples of common DEI initiatives that could be part of your strategy and how to put them in place. Don't think of this as a definitive list of the initiatives you should drive but think of them as examples to inspire your work.

Creating an employee inclusion and identity survey

An inclusion and identity survey is a good initiative to start with because it helps you better understand your organization. But it is not an initiative to undertake lightly. It requires a high level of DEI maturity and trust built up with your employees. It also requires the willingness of leadership to act on the results. A survey will help your organization find the baseline from where you are starting and give you the perspective to put the right initiatives in place.

The ability to combine identity data with responses to inclusion questions will allow you to understand how communities within your organization feel included or excluded. This is where the power of the inclusion and identity survey lies. But why is this important? If you just have an inclusion survey that has no questions around identity, it's impossible to understand how inclusion varies across the organization, specific to identity. Let's assume 75 percent of your organization feels included (based on their responses to a series of questions) and 25 percent do not feel included. If you don't know how identity intersects with inclusion, it's very difficult to uncover systemic issues of exclusion, bias or discrimination. Often the experiences of the majority (for example, white men) may mask the experiences of smaller communities within your company (such as Black women). You need to know more than just how the entire organization, in aggregate, feels. You will need to understand how *each* community within your organization feels.

Developing and launching an internal survey for your employees is an important but very complex task. It needs to be driven by someone who has the mandate (top-down) to do so and has the capacity to see it through. I wouldn't suggest driving it as a grassroots initiative. Addressing the results of the survey will require an organization-wide commitment to tackle the issues that arise. There are many key considerations from data privacy, legal barriers, stakeholder management, building trust and planning what you will do with the results of the survey. I've broken down the task of creating a global inclusion and identity employee survey into nine steps.

1. Figure out why you are doing the survey and what you will do with it

The first important step is to understand why you want to do such a survey. Collecting data for the sake of collecting data is not a good enough reason. When you ask people to share personal information with you, you are, in a way, creating a contract with them. You are telling them: "Please share this information with me and I will try to use it to make your experience and the experiences of others in our organization better." If you don't have an objective to use the results to make improvements, it's not fair to ask people to spend their time and energy to be vulnerable in answering the survey. Before you start this project, ask yourself and your organization: Why do we want this information? How will we use it to understand our organization better? How will we use it to improve our DEI work or to measure its impact? How and with whom will we share the results?

It's also essential to understand the landscape of trust around surveys in general in your organization. If your organization has conducted surveys in the past but they failed to result in meaningful action, it's difficult to build trust around a new survey on DEI. This trust is hard to build even if the motivations and intentions are different than from previous surveys. If this is your situation, organize focus groups to understand why there is not trust around the surveys and address those concerns before proceeding with a new inclusion and identity survey.

2. Make sure the Executive Team and HR are on board

Before you even start working on a survey, make sure you have the buy-in from the executive team and HR. This is a non-negotiable first step. Why? To achieve a high participation rate, you must have leaders throughout the organization who understand why you need the survey and are willing to encourage employees to take it. It's likely impossible to underestimate the value of having members of your executive team, ideally your CEO endorsing the survey. It is valuable in showing the strategic importance of the survey and the commitment you have made in conducting it.

HR, the internal communication team and other essential stakeholders need to fully understand *why* you will conduct this survey and what it will be used for. If you have key stakeholders that are not bought in, they may actually work against the success of your survey and potentially discourage people from taking it. Take the time to help everyone fully understand the purpose of the survey and its contribution to your DEI efforts. This stakeholder engagement step takes a deceptively long time to accomplish, so plan extra time for this.

3. Fully understand legal and privacy concerns

Anytime you are capturing sensitive, personal information related to identity (such as gender, race and ethnicity, sexuality, disability or other topics), you need to fully understand the risks involved. In Europe, GDPR has special considerations for this data which is outlined in Article 9: *Processing of special categories of personal data.*[1] According to GDPR, there are specific scenarios that allow the collection of Special Category data. One key scenario is that the employee taking the survey is fully informed and gives their consent (via a separate question in the survey) to provide their data, then the requirements of GDPR have been fulfilled. It's still important to responsibly collect and manage the data.

In addition to GDPR, some countries in Europe have their own laws and regulations regarding collecting employee data. Even if you are not subject to GDPR, your country may have other legal considerations for how to legally collect sensitive data. Some data categories may not be allowed. Be sure to consult with your local data protection and legal team (as well as external legal experts) to fully understand the legal restrictions in all relevant locations.

---

[1]GDPR Article 9: *https://gdpr-info.eu/art-9-gdpr/*

In addition to the legal considerations and to further protect employees and create trust in the survey, it's important to collect data in a way that ensures no survey administrator or other employee will ever be able to identify an individual through the results of the survey. When looking at the survey results, look at them only in aggregation, not at the individual level. This further protects you from individually identifying anyone. Using a threshold of a minimum number of survey results before you can view aggregated data also helps ensure you safeguard individuals' privacy. This threshold is minimally five but can be as high as 25.

Fully document all legal and privacy precautions including all the ways the data will be used before collecting any data. Include this documentation with the survey launch so employees are fully informed when they decide to participate. Most data regulations do not permit the use of collected data for purposes other than what has already been planned and communicated. Talk to your legal department and data privacy team to understand all of the concerns.

4. Find the right survey platform

Think about what survey platform you will use to administer the survey. You may already use a survey tool for employee surveys. If that's the case, evaluate it to see if it's appropriate for this type of survey. Some platforms will not allow the collection of sensitive data as part of an Inclusion and Identity survey, so be sure to check which types of surveys are possible in your preferred platform. There are also some survey platforms specializing in inclusion and identity surveys.[2]

An important benefit of working with a platform is collecting the data in an environment where it can be protected. Ideally, the platform you choose will have protections in place to make it impossible to view aggregated results that have not met a minimum threshold you define. This is a way to safeguard the data. Do not develop a survey without

---

[2]Platforms that specialize in Inclusion & Identity surveys: Peakon, CultureAmp, Pulsely. Though not specializing in these types of surveys, Glint is also a great option.

using a platform built specifically for employee surveys that can guarantee data privacy.[3]

Working with a platform that offers dashboards to visualize and filter data can offer more possibilities to analyze and interpret the results.

5. Design your survey

When designing a survey, think about what topics are most relevant and actionable for your organization. When you ask questions in a survey it's like creating a contract with your employees. You are asking for their experience, and you are committing to make improvements based on the results. If you ask questions without intending (or being able to) address those specific concerns, you will set expectations and then not follow through. So, think about what you can meaningfully change in your organization (or rather: *what is your organization willing to change?*).

Consider the length of your survey. Long, complex surveys may discourage participation. Instead, start with a shorter survey length of 5–10 questions for the identity topic and 5-10 questions for the inclusion topic. The survey itself and each individual question must be optional (no questions should be "required"). Some questions within the survey may need extra explanation, so plan to have supporting text within the survey to explain a specific question or terms you use.

Identity Questions

Regarding identity questions, there's, of course, a lot you could ask. Typical identity questions ask about: race and ethnicity, gender and transgender identity, sexual orientation, disability, parental status or caregiving responsibilities, tenure at the organization, refugee or migration status, age, religion, education level and languages spoken.

---

[3]Do not use Google Forms or any other basic survey platform that allows you to view individual survey results, even if anonymous. The risk of identification is too high.

You can also consider questions that help you better understand privilege, marginalization or access to resources, such as whether someone had financial support from family members to attend higher education or whether they received government assistance growing up. These questions can help you better understand whether your organization accepts and welcomes individuals who lack generational wealth and privilege.

Make sure every question you ask has a purpose and is meaningful to the DEI work you are doing. Do not ask every possible question just because you *can*. If you are not prepared to implement specific measures to increase representation and inclusion for the identity groups you are surveying about, do not ask.

Generally, identity questions should have a list of options to select from. For some questions, it's also helpful to have an open text field (for example race and ethnicity or sexual orientation questions). The open text field allows for self-identification beyond a defined list, which is an important part of giving people the agency and autonomy to declare their identity. But be thoughtful about when to add the open text field. Adding an open text field along with a question about disability may inadvertently encourage people to disclose medical information. Also, make sure each question has an option to select *I Prefer Not to Say*.

Inclusion Questions

Regarding inclusion questions, again, there's a lot you could ask. Typical inclusion questions ask about: sense of belonging, authenticity, leadership commitment, diversity of teams, role modeling of inclusive behavior, ability to voice diverse perspectives, fairness in compensation, discrimination or harassment in the workplace and equity of opportunities for growth or promotion. If you are working with a survey platform, they likely will have standard questions on different topics. They may also offer benchmarking, meaning for a specific question, they can compare the results of your organization to others. There are many blogs that offer drafts of inclusion, equity and belonging questions.[4] The appendix of this book also includes a comprehensive list of questions to consider.

So how to take the universe of possible questions and narrow it down to a first draft? With help from a focus group of trusted colleagues and stakeholders, discuss what questions are relevant and actionable for your organization. Use that insight to reduce the list of questions to a condensed first draft.

A small note about conducting a global survey: if your organization is located in several locations around the world, it takes extra work to develop a survey that is relevant and culturally sensitive in all locations. It may be necessary to make local adaptations of the survey. Be sure to get feedback from representatives in your organization across all sites. Don't simply take a standard identity survey administered in the US or the UK and apply it globally. You will need to adapt the language to be meaningful and culturally relevant. For translations, be sure to work with translators who are familiar with inclusive language to make sure the translations are locally appropriate.

6. Work with your communities

Before you finalize and launch the survey, work with your Employee Resource Groups and representatives from different locations and areas of your organization to get feedback on the survey's design. Reach out to any employee representation forums (works councils, etc.) to get their input (and sign-off if required by law). This is a crucial step to improve the quality and relevance of your survey. It also helps get key stakeholders engaged with the survey before it goes live. Specifically for your ERGs, it's important they feel like the survey is asking the right questions and

---

[4]Quantum Workplace: *https://www.quantumworkplace.com/future-of-work/diversity-and-inclusion-survey-questions*

Diversity in Tech: *https://www.diversityintech.co.uk/top-20-survey-questions-for-measuring-inclusion-at-work*

has the right purpose. Their participation is important, and they will only participate if they trust the survey and feel like it reflects their needs.

7. Communicate about the survey

Communication supporting the survey is an absolutely vital part of creating transparency and trust. This communication is not just for the average employee taking the survey but also for stakeholders critical to the survey's success, including HR, managers and your ERGs. If those stakeholders trust the survey, they are more likely to encourage others to take it. This communication should include an FAQ covering the following:

- the why (why are you doing the survey)
- the who (who was involved in creating the survey and who to talk to if you have concerns or questions)
- the what (what will the results be used for and what action is planned after the survey)

Communication should also cover common questions around privacy, such as who will have access to the results and how privacy is protected. Ask your stakeholders (leaders, DEI Council, HR, ERGs) to communicate directly about the survey and encourage participation. Invite your CEO to officially communicate the launch of the survey. This goes a long way in showing the strategic importance of the survey and increasing participation.

Plan your survey for a time in the year when there are no major disruptions (such as holiday seasons). Keep the survey open for two to three weeks to give employees the best chance to participate. Send a few reminders during the survey to help encourage participation.

8. Finding Meaningful Insight in the Results

The participation rate for an inclusion and identity survey will likely not be as high as regular employee engagement surveys. Understandably, there is more hesitancy around surveys that ask personal questions, so some employees will not wish to participate. Based on conversations with four European-based companies that have conducted Inclusion and Identity surveys in the past year, the average participation rate of the group was 58 percent. A participation rate above 50 percent will offer a more representative sample of the experiences of employees.

After you've administered the survey, look at results overall, by business area and by location. But importantly, see how the results for each question compare to results for specific communities. By using the results of the identity questions as a filter for the inclusion questions, you'll be able to see how your communities answered in comparison to your organization overall. For example, do parents feel less sense of belonging than non-parents? Do gay and lesbian employees feel less like they can be themselves at work compared to heterosexual colleagues?

Especially for small community groups, their experiences often get drowned out when looking at overall averages of data. The power of the survey comes from the ability to dive into the results at a community level. This helps you really understand the experiences of individual communities throughout your organization. The results of the survey can expose complex patterns. Sometimes you have to dig deeper to understand what's happening. Working with a data analyst will help you interrogate the data and ask the right questions. This process takes a lot of time to do accurately and comprehensively. It can also reveal some hard truths you need to deal with - which is part of the promise you make when you collect this data.

Be mindful of who has access to the full results. Even when your survey is entirely anonymous, if all managers have access to the results, some may be irresponsible or careless in interpreting them or acting upon them. Limit access to the survey results to a small pool of trusted stakeholders.

9. Communicating the results and acting

Plan to communicate the key insights of the survey back to your entire organization. This is part of the contract you make with your employees when you collect survey data. If the results show a lack of opportunity or inclusion for a specific community, meet directly with that community to understand the underlying issues. After you have had time to meet with stakeholders and reflect on the results, decide and communicate which initiatives you want to put in place to address the systemic issues you have identified in your organization. These initiatives should tie into the broader DEI strategy, but they may also require collaboration with other efforts in the company, such as hiring or compensation. Provide updates on the progress of those initiatives.

Final Thoughts

Your first inclusion and identity survey allows you to set a baseline and understand the climate of the organization. As your DEI work moves ahead, use the survey to track the progress of initiatives, such as a training initiative to support leaders to become more inclusive. You can assess if that initiative is having its intended impact by asking a question in your survey on whether managers role model inclusive behavior within the team. As you move ahead, you may want to add questions to address other concerns or adapt questions to make them more clear. Remember, employees experience survey fatigue if they are constantly asked questions but never see change happen. Acting on the results is one of the most important aspects of the survey.

In summary, below are the four most critical elements of success for an inclusion and identity survey:

1. A platform that will protect the privacy of your employees and not allow individual identification. Ideally, the platform will allow you to look at survey results for subsets of your employees, for example, based on their location, business unit or identity group.

2. Strong buy-in from key stakeholders such as HR and legal who understand the purpose of the survey and support the project.

3. Collaboration with your ERGs to develop a relevant survey that addresses their needs along with a commitment to share the relevant results with them.

4. A clear, top-down endorsement from your CEO and executive team that the survey is part of a strategic focus on DEI. This makes sure the survey is perceived as a company-wide business-critical effort.

The entire process of survey development and stakeholder engagement can be really time-consuming. You will likely receive a lot of feedback and concerns from your stakeholders. Take the feedback you receive to heart. Even if there are no legal considerations, there may still be cultural considerations that influence how you design and launch the survey. Remind yourself why you are doing the survey and what you are trying to achieve. In some cases, it may be better to compromise on the scope of questions in order to get overall buy-in for the survey and encourage participation!

Embedding DEI work through an advocate program

One of the biggest challenges of implementing a broad DEI strategy is to create accountability throughout the organization, so the strategy becomes truly embedded. I've seen a lot of situations where the impact and ownership of DEI is limited to HR, with no accountability across other areas of the organization. This makes it very easy for employees and business leaders to ignore or dismiss the work. One way to embed the strategy is to make sure it is ranked highly among company-wide strategic initiatives and business leaders are personally accountable to implement DEI in their area of the business. To supplement this, you can create a network of advocates throughout the organization that can locally drive the DEI work in a way that is relevant to those business areas and locations.

Why is it important for your global strategy to be locally relevant? A DEI strategy will not automatically serve the needs of *all* locations of a global organization. DEI means different things in different countries. Each location will require different efforts locally. Similarly, in a large organization, especially following many mergers and restructurings, each business area will have developed its own culture and challenges. An advocate program will help you address those challenges by adapting your strategy.

To be clear, an advocate program is not a replacement for an organization hiring someone to drive DEI work centrally. It's also not a quick-fix solution. It's a step to take, after the strategy is created, in order to create ownership for that strategy across the organization and make sure it is locally relevant.

Introducing the advocate program

An advocate program is a structure for empowering individuals throughout the organization to take ownership of and implement some aspect of the company-wide DEI strategy locally within their area of the business or their geographic location. An advocate program offers a process to onboard new advocates, upskill them and offer recognition for doing the work. An advocate program is specifically helpful for an organization with a global strategy and locations in many different countries. But it's also beneficial for an organization that is big and decentralized, meaning there are several business areas with their own challenges and goals.

Though there may be some overlap in interest, DEI advocates are not the same as ERG organizers. The purpose of advocate work is specifically to implement strategic DEI initiatives locally. DEI advocates also should not be considered volunteers. This work is very much strategic work and should be recognized officially. Lastly, DEI advocates willingly step forward to take on this work, but they are not rogue agents driving their own pet projects. The most important is that their efforts are aligned with the overarching DEI strategy with a reporting mechanism to keep the DEI team and local stakeholders informed.

Ideally, the advocate roles are filled through a lightweight selection process to make sure you have the right skills and locations represented. A DEI advocate should be interested in DEI work and have the project management skills to drive local initiatives with relative autonomy. The local business leaders should also be fully informed and signed off on their location's involvement in the advocate program. Getting that buy-in takes time and requires stakeholder management to explain the goals of the program. The local business area will also need to agree that a percentage of the advocate's work time can be spent on this.

Equip advocates with skills and awareness

Most importantly, DEI Advocates need to be fully fluent in the overarching DEI strategy and understand its goals and initiatives. This requires onboarding, including a workshop or some 1:1 time with the DEI team to understand the strategy fully. DEI advocates should be aware of the immediate priorities and long-term goals of the strategy and any metrics that the DEI team tracks. It's also imperative for the advocates to understand what's out of scope for this role. Local DEI advocates should not be considered a local ombudsman for harassment reporting or a catchall for complaints or new ideas. The purpose of the advocate role is to bring the global strategy to a local level.

Advocates, of course, also need a strong foundational understanding of DEI concepts and best practices. A learning curriculum for virtual or in-person training courses is useful as well as a reading list. Advocates will also have situations arise where they don't have the answers, so it's important that the DEI team or other experts are accessible to help them in problem-solving. An efficient way to support this would also be to offer office hours with the DEI team or a chat room for the advocates to support each other in peer problem-solving.

Align local efforts with a global strategy

DEI advocates offer a bridge between broader, global efforts and local needs. The role of the advocate begins with investigating what those local needs are. Do this by looking at local survey results and talking with local leaders or ERG chapters organizers. Find out if there are any local DEI initiatives already in progress that would potentially fall under the remit of the DEI advocate work.

The next step becomes adapting the broader strategy by selecting initiates to roll out locally. Here are a few examples of what this could look like:

- If the broader strategy includes a goal towards inclusive language in communication, a local initiative could develop an inclusive language guide in the local language or host training that addresses how inclusive language is relevant for the specific business.

- If the tech business area identifies a difficulty hiring women and a need to identify and mitigate bias from their hiring process, the advocate could launch a project to review and improve hiring processes in tech as well as a plan to reach out to industry-relevant job boards.

It's important that advocate work is in line with the broader strategy to make sure that everyone is working towards achieving the same goals. But it's also important to realize that there's no one-size-fits-all solution. Adapting the DEI strategy to local needs is necessary to achieve broad success. Regular communication between the advocates and the DEI team makes sure that everyone is working in sync.

Reporting success

Regularly (monthly or quarterly), the network of advocates can get together with the DEI team to provide updates on what they're working on to support the goals of the strategy. This includes updates of ongoing initiatives or reporting on relevant program metrics. These regular meetings are a critical moment to make sure that the advocates are able to have the intended impact through the local efforts they are driving. Make this progress visible to local business stakeholders so they can see the impact of the advocates.

Recognize and compensate advocates' work

The most direct recognition of advocates' work is to make sure it is considered part of their work time, not volunteer time. Local stakeholders, as well as the DEI team, must perceive this work *as work*. Managers will need to show their support by adjusting workloads to accommodate the work. Depending on the scope of work, 10-20 percent of working time is probably a reasonable starting point. Revisit this based on feedback from the advocates on whether it's sufficient to achieve local goals. Additionally, this work should be recognized during performance reviews. You can also create visibility of the work with a badge on their employee intranet profile or in the employee's email signature.

Reflect on impact

The ultimate objective is for the advocates to contribute to the goals of the strategy by driving local initiatives. Check in periodically to make sure that is happening. If it's not, take a pause and refocus.

I hope you notice a theme in this book that DEI work cannot be driven by one single person. It has to truly be embedded throughout the organization with local drivers and accountability in place. This advocate program is one piece of practically making that happen, especially in a large or widespread organization.

Launching a holistic diversity hiring program

Based on my experience talking to organizations eager to get started on DEI, the number one initiative they want to launch is "diversity hiring". But you may notice I haven't mentioned it much in this book thus far. That is because I don't recommend it as the initial focus of your efforts. But, why? Simply put, if your organization is not yet inclusive and welcoming to a diverse workforce, then focusing on "diversity hiring" initiatives is just setting yourself and your new hires up for a lot of disappointment and harm. So many organizations spend a lot of time and money on these initiatives, but they don't first look at their internal culture and processes to understand what it's like for employees once they are hired.

The reality is: hiring does not exist in a vacuum. A successful hiring strategy requires a holistic approach that includes putting intentional processes in place and creating a working environment that is safe and inclusive. Hiring for diversity is not as simple as getting applicants through the door. It is not one initiative; it's a series of interconnected initiatives. These initiatives build onto one another to create a solid and successful approach. Let's dive in.

What do you want to achieve, and what's working against you?

Before you kick off any hiring initiatives, think about what you are trying to achieve. What does a diverse organization look like for you, in your industry, in your locations? If you already have data on the diversity of your workforce, great. If not, it makes sense first to collect this through a survey before you get started; otherwise, it's difficult to know where you are starting from and whether you are making progress. Measuring progress will become an important indicator of success.

Next, think about what internal processes, workplace culture and baggage[5] will work *against* your efforts. Start with the results of your D&I survey or employee engagement surveys. Do they provide insight on what the employee experience is like, especially for employees who are part of marginalized communities? If you don't have this data, set up focus groups with your ERGs to understand what challenges they faced and whether they'd recommend the working environment as it currently is. Do they feel they have opportunities for growth and progression that would entice them to stay? And importantly, look at exit surveys to

---

[5]By baggage, I mean "skeletons in the closet." This could include complaints of inequality, allegations against senior leaders, toxic personalities in leadership, issues with harassment or discrimination or any other workplace culture issues that have not been dealt with. These affect the wellbeing of your employees and hurt the credibility of your work.

understand *why* people leave your organization. Check glassdoor to see how employees who left *really* feel.

If you have issues with inequitable processes, exclusionary work environments or lack of buy-in among leaders, you need to spend time fixing those issues before kicking off hiring initiatives. Otherwise, you are inviting people to join an organization that is not welcoming or inclusive; in the end, you will cause more harm than if you had done nothing at all. While you are in your planning phase, take some time to talk to your recruiters and hiring managers to see what challenges they face in hiring a diverse workforce and where they see opportunities for improvement.

Think about how your organization looks from the outside

Today, many job seekers are looking for organizations that prioritize diversity when considering where to apply.[6] From their perspective, it can be challenging to figure out if an organization truly cares about diversity, equity and inclusion or just tells a convincing story. Take a moment to put yourself in the role of a job seeker. Imagine you know nothing of your organization. Look at your external communication, glassdoor reviews, Twitter posts and news articles. Ask yourself: Is your organization highlighting its DEI work? Are you sharing clear commitments with accountability measures? Do ERGs have a voice in the communication? If you need some inspiration, look around at your competitors in the industry. How are they telling an authentic story about their DEI efforts? Remember, job seekers have their pick among the best organizations in the world. You need to convince *them* your organization should be among their top choice.

The next step is looking at your job postings. In collaboration with your Talent team, develop a diversity statement that explains your views on DEI and your commitments in an authentic way. Make sure

---

[6]For younger job seekers, diversity and inclusion in the workplace aren't a preference. They're a requirement. *https://www.washingtonpost.com/business/2021/02/18/millennial-genz-workplace-diversity-equity-inclusion/*

this is included in the template for all job ads that are posted. When writing the statement, be bold but speak the truth, don't write anything you cannot stand behind. Ask your ERGs to review the text for authenticity. To add context and credibility, link to blogs or published reports that further explain your DEI commitment. Remember to be inclusive beyond binary gender and think about the full potential of diversity in your industry and within your workforce. The appendix contains an example of a diversity statement that can be adapted for your job postings.

Next, read your job postings for bias. There are tools[7] that can do this for you. But an even better approach is to ask for feedback from a diverse panel of colleagues on how they perceive the job posting and whether it sounds exciting and welcoming to them. Here are specific considerations for a well-written, attractive job posting:

1. Read the "required" skills and experience section and ask yourself, *are all of these needed?* Overfilling the requirements may discourage some applicants from applying.

2. Include a salary range in the job post. This shows you value transparency and fairness in compensation and want to give as much information as possible to help applicants decide whether the role is right for them.

3. Set clear expectations by explaining what support you offer and what you don't. Include whether you sponsor working permits for international workers or support remote working or flexible scheduling. Include information on any benefits or policies you have that would encourage applicants to apply (such as stipends for home office equipment, education budgets, medical support for non-married partners and any mental health or wellness offerings).

4. Make sure applicants have a way to learn more about your organization and the team by including a link to your website.

---

[7]For example: *Text.io* and Gender Decoder: *http://gender-decoder.katmatfield.com/*

This helps how job seekers decide whether they can picture themselves working with you.

5. Provide information on how the hiring process works and what to expect. List the interview stages, additional information that will be requested and whether feedback will be offered during the process. This, again, offers transparency and increases interest in applying. Be sure you stick to the processes you communicate.

You may think that hiring is about your organization finding the employee that is right for you. That's only half of the picture. It's also about an applicant finding out if your organization is right for them. Every word in your communication is an opportunity to authentically show your values and commitments.

Build meaningful, mutually beneficial relationships

If your current employees feel included and appreciated, they are more likely to recommend your organization to their friends and family. You can consider a paid referral program, specifically for ERG members, to encourage employees to refer their contacts for open roles. If you do go this referral route, make sure your recruiters give proper attention to these applicants.

Externally, relationships and partnerships are also important. ERG members likely know the relevant professional networks[8] for your industry. Partnering with those networks and groups is an excellent way to reach more applicants. But partnering should not be limited to a financial donation. Think about how you can genuinely support these groups to help them fulfill their own goals. For example, you could offer a space for their events, mentoring and resume reviews for their

---

[8]Examples of identity based professional networks: Persian Women in Tech, Unicorns in Tech (A Global LGBTIQ+ Tech Community), Latinx in Publishing, ADAN (Afro Deutsches Akademiker Netzwerk).

members or collaborating on a project together. A good partnership should be mutually beneficial to your organization and the network.

Another option to reach a wider audience is to use specialized diversity job boards.[9] There are many to check out; often they are industry, community or location specific. The fees for posting vary, so consider reviewing multiple platforms to see what fits your needs best. One last option would be partnering with a diversity sourcing agency that can help connect you directly to applicants.[10]

Put strong hiring processes in place

So, by now, hopefully, you have a lot of great applicants but are you actually making good, unbiased decisions? Take some time to think about the lifecycle of your applicant experience including what information they are asked to share, who first contacts them, how many interviews they have, who conducts the interviews, who makes the decision to hire and how is the compensation offer decided. All of these processes have the potential to introduce bias or discrimination or just simply alienate applicants. The first step is to map out the entire journey and who is the owner for each step. How long is the entire hiring process? Are you losing good candidates because the process takes too long? Next, look at each step of the process and assess for bias and inclusion. To support inclusive recruitment and hiring processes, you can create a checklist for recruiters and hiring managers to follow while conducting resume reviews and interviewing. There are many examples of these checklists online.[11] In general, the checklist should cover the steps the hiring manager and recruiter should take to ensure an inclusive

---

[9]For example: _https://diversity-jobs.de/_, _https://www.diversityinresearch.careers/_, _https://www.blackcareernetwork.com/_

[10]For example: _https://talentdiverse.com/_, _http://www.talentinternational.com/_, _https://www.diversifytech.co/work-with-us_

[11]For example: _https://www.hrmorning.com/wp-content/uploads/2020/11/JazzHR-Inclusive-Recruitment-PDF.pdf_ and _https://rework.withgoogle.com/guides/unbiasing-use-structure-and-criteria/steps/use-unbiasing-checklists/_

hiring process. This would include an explanation of common types of bias and how to avoid them, instructions on how to reach a diverse applicant pool and shortlist, what topics to avoid in interviews and how to create an inclusive setting while interviewing. Once you create the checklist, make sure it's being used and stays up to date.

Here are additional tips that can help reduce bias and create a better, more inclusive experience for your applicants:

- Proactively ask applicants not to include a photo or any family information on their resume.[12]

- Conduct initial reviews of the applications blind by removing names and other identifying information from the applications.

- Develop a standard set of questions to ask applicants, which helps avoid bias introduced by assessing each applicant differently.

- Avoid take-home assignments or tests as part of the interview process. Those extra assignments disadvantage applicants that don't have a lot of free time due to personal or family obligations.

- Make sure the team conducting the interviews is diverse and has been trained in recognizing bias.

- Consider adding a cultural interview that includes specific questions about the applicant's understanding of DEI concepts and how inclusion and equity fit within their work.

When it finally comes to making a decision, wait to make a hiring decision until you have a diverse list of shortlisted applicants. Use a standard approach for comparing finalists systematically (for example, a scoring rubric) to avoid "gut feeling" decisions. Consider having an independent talent panel who can objectively assess candidates without

---

[12]It's common in Germany for resumes to include photos and personal family information (such as marital status). Some companies actively discourage applicants from including this as it introduces bias as seen this research: Weichselbaumer, Doris (2016) Discrimination against Female Migrants Wearing Headscarves, IZA Discussion Papers, No. 10217, Institute for the Study of Labor (IZA), Bonn. https://www.econstor.eu/bitstream/10419/147903/1/dp10217.pdf

the urgency bias the hiring manager may have.[13] When it comes time to make an offer of compensation, have a planned salary range for each role. Tie the position within the range to the percentage of qualifications of the role the applicant has met. In terms of equitable compensation, keep in mind the salaries for existing employees in the same role. If the standard market-rate salary increases faster than internal raises, you may have new, potentially more junior, employees making more than existing employees. If this begins to happen, adjust the salaries of current employees right away; otherwise, salary inequality grows over time.

And lastly, to create transparency among employees, make sure all hired employees have job descriptions that are transparent to them and their team. In some cases, these will evolve, but be sure to document them as they do.

Measure the impact of your efforts

Tracking your progress helps you understand whether your work is having any impact. This is often an overlooked step because it is *hard to do*. Consider all the hiring-related initiatives you have implemented. Are the initiatives effective in different departments and locations? For example, if you've developed a hiring checklist, is it being consistently used?

To understand the impact of your efforts, you'll need to look at the applications coming in and the different stages of the pipeline to see how applicants move through the system and whether you are actually hiring a more diverse workforce. The most straightforward way to do this is to have an optional, short survey during the application stage that collects personal data (such as gender, race, nationality). This data can be aggregated and reviewed at each stage to see if some identity groups are being excluded throughout the process. This helps you understand if you have further issues of bias or exclusion at some part of the process.

---

[13]Learn about the "Bar Raiser" process in the chapter *Hiring* in *Working Backwards* by Colin Bryar and Bill Carr.

Another essential thing to track is retention. How long are your existing and new employees staying? If they leave, why? This is an important way to understand whether you have other unknown issues. The inclusion survey, discussed in Part 5: *Creating an employee inclusion and identity survey*, can also help you understand how inclusion varies by community, location or area of the business.

Final thoughts on inclusive hiring

There are entire books written about inclusive hiring practices. So please consider this an inspirational jumping-off point, not a fully comprehensive program. Your organization, industry, location and where you are starting from will significantly impact your approach. Also, keep in mind that your efforts are also dependent on many other internal factors beyond the actual hiring. This includes how inclusive your culture is (building an inclusive workplace is covered in-depth in Part 6: *Deep Dive: Creating Inclusion in the Workplace*) and whether your organization has strong retention and opportunity for growth.

Lastly, a very important thing to note: if your organization is making decisions around succession planning, layoffs, promotions or restructurings without thinking about the intersection between those decisions and the diversity hiring work, there is a considerable risk of deeply undermining your efforts and spoiling goodwill. Here's a story to put this into perspective: a major airport implemented a program to hire Deaf employees to work in their baggage handling department. They hired Sign Language interpreters to translate and arranged a personal vibrating alarm system to protect Deaf employees in the case of emergencies. The program was hugely successful and won the airport an award for disability inclusion in the workplace. Less than 6 months later, due to the impact of Covid and the implementation of new automation technology, the airport laid off ⅓ of its baggage handling staff including all the Deaf employees (as they were new to the company and first in line for layoffs). The team driving the accessibility initiative was not consulted or included in any of the decisions regarding downsizing. This is just one story, but there are many examples of how well-meaning DEI efforts are undermined by siloed decisions taken elsewhere in the organization. Take a moment to step back from your ambitions around hiring and ask yourself: *what other processes and risk factors stand in the way of your success?* Diversity hiring work does not exist in a vacuum of isolation. It is interconnected with every single other employed-related decision.

Identifying and cultivating meaningful partnerships

Likely at some point along your organization's DEI journey, you will want to set up a partnership with an external organization. Partnerships can help you achieve your goals through a mutually beneficial and supportive relationship. Simultaneously, that partnership will also support the external organization in pursuing its own goals and objectives. This section is all about how to identify the right partnerships and make the most of them.[14]

What is a partnership?

Partnerships can unlock new opportunities to support your goals in your strategy. They can help you work towards your diversity commitments or contribute to building a more inclusive working environment. Simultaneously, a successful partnership also helps the organization achieve its own goals through growth, connections or funding.

A successful partnership has clear goals for both you and the organization you are partnering with. From the outset, it's important to mutually set expectations on what you want to do together and how you will support each other. Ideally, you share a common interest, which means your two individual paths are both leading towards a similar destination. Throughout this collaboration, one key element is the trust you build up over time between your two organizations. This trust means

---

[14]The concept for this section was suggested by one of the early readers of this book, Jessica Gedamu. The section was inspired by conversations with Helene Mathelemuse and Vanessa Sanyauke.

you keep the others' interests in mind and you both plan to accomplish the work you've set out to do.

When picturing a partnership, think strategically, not short-term. When you think long-term, the time and money investment go further and you have more time to build up a trusting relationship and ultimately have a bigger impact than you could with short-term relationships. Practically this means that instead of supporting a one-off event, think about how you could collaborate with an organization to support your long-term goals while supporting their organization to grow.

What do growth and maturity look like for the organization you are partnering with? Sometimes partnering with an organization supports them to expand and grow their organization beyond your relationship, sometimes even reaching new partners or unlocking new opportunities for them. This could be through connections you make to other companies to partner with, the brand recognition they are able to gain through your partnership, the ability for them to grow their staff based on financial investment or maturing their organization to expand their scope.

For your organization, partnerships are also an important element of reputation building. There is always well-deserved criticism of companies that focus on DEI just for branding and marketing. Collaborating on a mutually beneficial partnership with a respected organization gives you a chance to tell an authentic story of how you supported them to achieve their goals, while also achieving your own goals.

Where to find partners?

First, identify what topics you want to work on as defined by your strategy. Think about and document how exactly a partnership with an external organization could support you in achieving your goals. Organizations that fit that criteria will likely be non-profits, universities, community organizations or social enterprises. To find the right partner, look internally to see if you have any contacts among your employees.

Your ERGs will be a key connector here. If you have some recommendations, make sure those organizations also can support you in achieving your goals. A strongly recommended potential partner still needs to help you get where you want to go.

Also, conduct your own research on organizations that are topically and locally relevant. Organizations may also reach out to you directly. These organizations, particularly those that are supporting marginalized communities, may not have the network connections that make it possible to get warm introductions to their potential partners. Reaching out directly may be their only option. It's worth considering these partners if they are a good match for you and what you would like to achieve.

What criteria to consider when evaluating a partnership?

Here are five things to consider to find an organization that is the right fit for your partnership:

1. **Create basic governance:** Even if it's your first partnership, more requests and opportunities will come along. It's worth taking some time to put governance in place to document how you review new opportunities for partnership, what criteria must be met and who must be involved in the decision. This governance can evolve over time as you make more decisions but it's always good to start with something brief and workable.

2. **Do your homework:** Next, document what you want to achieve with the partnership, how long you expect the partnership to last and how much time and money you are able to contribute. It's OK to start small and build up the ambition for the partnership over time as you see the impact it's having and you build up mutual trust.

3. **Talk with them:** Have an open conversation to understand what your potential partner wants to achieve. This is where it becomes critical to find a partner that's not just looking to find a

pot of funding, but an organization that wants to create something collaboratively and organically together.

4. **Think beyond your immediate focus:** A good partnership has the potential to have an impact on the broader geographic area or industry where you are working. This could involve using a partnership to set new standards or guidelines for others in your industry or offering resources many can benefit from. A good partnership may also impact other strategic goals your organization has beyond DEI, including sustainability, corporate citizenship, branding or developing new business relationships. From the beginning, having stakeholders from other parts of your organization in the room can help you identify opportunities to collaborate further.

5. **Conduct due diligence:** With the support of your legal team, conduct a compliance check by reviewing the financial records and past press of the organization. Identify any concerns and reach out to the organization directly to resolve any open questions before proceeding with the partnership.

Remember that simultaneously your potential partner is also vetting you and is reading the press about your organization as well. This relationship you want to build needs to extend beyond your shared goals to make sure you are aligned on values and reputation too.

How to measure the success of a partnerships

For a successful partnership, both parties need to have their goals met. In order to measure success, first document the goals and objectives you each have. Ideally, you can quantify these goals to make them measurable. Data will become key to understanding the impact the partnership has in achieving your goals. Depending on the partnership this could be: the number of job applicant leads generated through a jointly hosted event, number of hires and long-term retention of those hires, number of blog posts co-published, number of webinars recorded or resources generated for your community. This is really dependent on the goals of your partnership. Commit to measuring these goals on a regular basis. By tracking progress over time, you can see how your partnership is evolving. And if you have multiple partnerships with a similar goal, you can compare the outcome of one to another.

At the end of the first year of the partnership, have a check-in with your partner organization and ask them how they think the partnership is going. Has it helped them achieve their goals? Have they identified other opportunities to collaborate? Setting aside some budget to be flexible to support a new opportunity that arises for you or your partner can further build that long-term relationship and help your partner to be agile in their programming as well.

Based on best practices to make the most out of successful partnerships, I've proposed some principles:

- **Think strategically and long-term** in order to build a relationship with real impact. Focusing on just one collaboration or event (considering all the evaluation and due diligence that goes into that initial commitment) means you have invested a lot of initial work for a short-lived partnership. Thinking long-term helps you get a lot more out of the investment and may be truly transformational for an organization that is growing over time.

- **A good partnership is truly mutually beneficial**. This means you are both getting something valuable from the partnership. What does this practically look like? Let's say your organization is seeking better connections to a specific community for hiring or recruiting and an external organization is really able to make that connection. If they are also able to build their proposition in strategic hiring markets and their reputation as collaborating with large organizations, you are both benefiting from this partnership. This is where the elusive mutually beneficial partnership lies, exactly at the intersection where you are helping each other achieve your goals.

- **Make sure you have the right people in the room** to unlock doors (within your own organization or for your partner). This could include talent acquisition, employer branding, ERGs, Communications as well as senior leaders. Take the time to understand how these stakeholders can be valuable to your partnership and make sure they are a part of the conversation early on, especially if they are critical to its success.

- **Plan and budget annually, with flexibility** for reactionary opportunities. Before the start of the next year, decide how much money you want to invest in your partnership relationships. This helps you plan ahead and gives you a chance to set expectations with partners. In addition to your annual budgeting, set aside some buffer of budget for situations or requests you need to react to with short notice. This could be in response to a world event or crisis. If this situation impacts the communities of your ERGs, make sure they have a chance to give input in how this money can support their communities. If you don't proactively set aside money for this, you may end up depleting your planned annual budget for partnerships before you have the chance to collaborate.

- **Regular communication and time investment** from your side. A good partnership does not just require an investment of money. You need to plan to invest the time to make the most of your partnerships. This could include getting different stakeholders involved, tracking data and communicating on a regular basis. In How to hire a DEI consultant in Part 2, we also talked about the commitment required from your side for a successful consultant relationship. Partnerships are no different. It requires ongoing engagement and involvement. It's not just a financial transaction.

- **Understand the dependencies of the partnership.** A common pitfall in DEI work is not thinking holistically about the initiatives we're doing. We tend to have a narrow focus (for example on talent attraction) and seek a partner that will just offer solutions on that topic. But there are so many interdependencies to something like hiring. If your organization is not inclusive and you have low retention or poor professional progression, you are welcoming new employees to join your organization just for them to leave shortly after. For a partner who focuses on talent, they don't want to send their community to a company with a bad culture. Before going all-in on a partnership, think about all the other dependencies that may undermine your efforts. Some of these you probably have control over, while others you won't.

- **Think creatively and think big.** A partnership could be used to bring together other organizations in your industry for an even greater impact. Vanessa Sanyauke of Girls Talk London[15] shared with me the success she had in building a partnership across four telecom companies: O2, BT, Vodafone and Ericsson.[16] Instead of just focusing on one organization, she harnessed an opportunity to partner industry-wide to truly have a greater impact. By collaborating across organizations, Girls Talk London was able to provide mentors to 186 girls, some of whom went on to further education at global institutions such as MIT and Oxford University or took on roles at Virgin Media O2 and BT.

Final thoughts

Partnerships cannot solve 100% of everything you are trying to achieve. They will not be able to handle all of your recruiting needs or magically transform your organization into an inclusive one. But they can help you move the dial in a positive direction if you invest the right amount of time and energy. And, in some cases, a good partner can even function

---

[15]Girls Talk London: *https://www.girlstalklondon.com/*
[16]Learn more about this partnership here:
https://www.capacitymedia.com/article/29v4sbvyhu4ymjql54934/big-interview/girls-talk-london-diversifying-the-telco-pipeline

almost as an extension of your organization. Especially when it's a group of people you collaborate with, share goals with and truly trust.

PART 6:
DEEP DIVE: CREATING INCLUSION IN THE WORKPLACE

Inclusion deserves its own chapter in this book so we can fully explore what it practically means in the workplace.

What is inclusion? As described earlier: Inclusion means creating an organizational culture where people feel comfortable to be themselves and bring their differences to the table; where they feel valued and welcome, especially if they're different from the majority. Inclusion is needed, especially for a diverse workforce, because it ensures everyone, no matter who they are, is heard and able to contribute. Inclusion is for everyone, but we also need to ask ourselves, who do we want to feel the impact of our work? Let's be clear here, when we talk about inclusion in the workplace, we must prioritize our efforts to increase the inclusion for individuals who are not the majority in the organization. The majority already benefits from the safety and comfort of seeing many people around them that look like themselves.

What does it mean when employees feel a sense of inclusion? It means employees show up to work and feel welcome to be there. It means they feel like they can voice their opinion, even if it contradicts their teammates or managers, and their opinion will be *listened* to. It means they can share information about their lives without fear of judgment. It means the organization has made the extra effort to listen to and anticipate the needs of those employees and create a workplace where they don't have to constantly ask for (and be denied) the small and big things they need to feel welcome.

What does this practically look like? For a Muslim employee, it could mean having a place to pray in the workplace designed with their needs in mind. For a queer woman, it could mean not having to correct assumptions about their life (for example being assumed to have a boyfriend or husband). For a Person of Color, it could mean having the feeling of safety and wellbeing and not facing microaggressions or othering in the workplace.[1]

But how do you know whether employees feel included? The easiest thing is to *ask them*. This can be done in an employee survey (see *Creating an employee inclusion and identity survey* in Part 5) that asks specific

---

[1] "Othering" refers to the process whereby an individual or groups of people attribute negative characteristics to other individuals or groups of people that set them apart as representing that which is opposite to them. It refers to more than just stereotyping, as this can involve making generalizations about groups of people which may be positive or negative. *Encyclopedia of Critical Psychology. Springer, New York, NY.* https://doi.org/10.1007/978-1-4614-5583-7_414

questions about experiences or feelings that contribute to inclusion. Here are some example questions:

- In my team, people's ideas are judged on their quality, not on the personal characteristics of those who express them.
- I feel comfortable being myself at work.
- I feel respected by my colleagues and manager.
- I am included in decisions that affect my work.
- There are leaders in my organization that I can relate to.

It's more important to understand how employees who are *not in the majority* and not represented in leadership feel included or excluded. If instead, you look at the average level of inclusion for all employees together regardless of identity, you'll have an incomplete picture. This is especially true if your workplace is not particularly diverse because the experiences of minority and underrepresented employees will be drowned out by the average experiences of individuals who are in the majority. If you don't have immediate plans for a survey, another option would be to have a series of discussions with your ERGs and ask them how they feel and what challenges they face.

Let's now talk about *how* to create an inclusive workplace and how to put intentional programs and reminders in place so everyone is accountable and contributes to an inclusive workplace.

Inclusive onboarding

It's natural to start with onboarding because it's one of the first times a new employee interacts with your organization. This first experience shows the employee what your organization cares about and sets expectations for future interactions.

What is inclusive onboarding?

Employee onboarding is the process of welcoming new colleagues to your organization. This involves sharing the culture and values of the organization and providing context to the new colleague to help them understand the specifics of their role. Onboarding also offers practical information, training and tools needed to get the job done. It's an essential opportunity for the new joiner to ask questions and get to know their new team.

At larger organizations, onboarding is typically a clearly defined process with many interactions between the new employee and the organization. Starting a new job is already stressful and creates a lot of uncertainty and anxiety. Providing a very clear onboarding experience helps resolve that stress and uncertainty.

Inclusive onboarding takes onboarding to the next level. An inclusive onboarding experience accommodates and supports all your new employees, not just some of them. As a result, new employees receive the support they need to get settled and ultimately feel welcome in the organization. Inclusive onboarding is not about constructing a checklist of behaviors or accommodations to make. Instead, it's about listening to your employees to understand their needs and developing a program that makes sure they are seen and heard. Below are the three main stages of onboarding and examples of inclusive initiatives for each part.

Before Day 1

New employees are interacting with and learning about their new employer before their first day on the job. This is often called the pre-onboarding phase.

Relocation Support

For employees that are relocating for the job, think about what their needs are. Supporting them in obtaining a work permit (if necessary), finding housing, understanding local bureaucracy and getting settled is a huge help. Provide customized support to those who need extra help in relocation, for example:

- Employees with families

- Employees with disabilities
- Employees who care for family members (for example, a parent)
- Employees with religious observances that require dietary restrictions or specific prayer times
- Employees who do not speak the local language

Regarding financial support for relocation, in Europe, relocation can cost somewhere between 2,000 and 10,000 euros. A system that requires the employee to pay all the costs for relocation in advance and then wait for a reimbursement can be very exclusionary for individuals without significant financial assets. Consider providing financial relocation support in advance.

Guide to a New City

Depending on the city in question, relocation can be complicated by layers of bureaucracy and paperwork. Try to make this process as easy as possible to alleviate that mental burden for the new employee. This can include instructions or support to "register" (if needed) with the local government office, obtain a bank account, get tax identification information, find an apartment and sign a rental contract.

Beyond bureaucracy, providing additional information about the new city helps make settlement easier. This includes sharing information about:

- How to enroll children in childcare or school
- Location of cultural institutions and religious spaces
- How to get in touch with police or other emergency services
- How to find medical care such as general practitioners or specialty doctors (especially in an emergency)
- Health and community spaces including those that offer special healthcare such as HIV+ support, PrEP, STD testing and counseling
- Queer and LGBTQI+ community spaces

- Spaces that provide mental health support

This isn't an exhaustive list. Ask your current employees what they had to sort out on their own when they relocated and use that for inspiration to create support documents for new employees. Your ERGs may also be able to contribute information and resources that are relevant to their communities.

Welcome from the Team

Make sure the colleague's new team reaches out before day one. This creates a bit of psychological safety before that intimidating first day at a new job. If any team-building events are scheduled shortly before the new employee's start date, make sure the team extends an invitation.

During Week One

The first week at a new job can be very stressful. It's a time of uncertainty where everything is unfamiliar. This list of initiatives aims to make that first week as easy and welcoming as possible.

Site maps

For on-site (non-remote) roles, office campuses can be confusing to navigate. For a new employee, everything is unfamiliar; getting around can be particularly stressful. Provide employees with site maps to show them the layout of the buildings, meeting rooms and important social places like the cafeteria or lounge. Be sure to add inclusion sites such as accessible entrances, inclusive bathrooms, prayer rooms, parent-child rooms, quiet spaces, relaxation rooms, first aid rooms and anything else relevant for your space. Even if the employee doesn't need to use all of those spaces, they will know about them and can share information with others.

Employee Resource Groups

If your organization has Employee Resource Groups, make sure these are visible from day one. This is a great way to help new employees build their communities from the beginning of their time with your organization. Make sure the steps to create a *new* ERG are clear and accessible.

Names & Pronouns

Consider the need for employees to use a name different from what's on their legal documents. This name would be used for all internal communication including email and profile accounts. To understand this more, learn about deadnaming[2] and what this can mean for the trans (short for transgender) community. If you enable a flexible names policy, it is not simply an administrative process to put in place but a way to acknowledge and recognize trans identity. Employees who are not trans also benefit from having a flexible names policy as many people do not use their legal names for various reasons. Additionally, encouraging all new (and current) employees to proactively share their pronouns and use the correct pronouns of others is a great way to welcome people to feel seen.

Buddy System

Put a buddy system in place to provide psychological safety for a new employee. This makes sure new employees always have someone they can go to with questions as they are acclimating to their new role and perhaps a new city. This buddy relationship can be one piece of a powerful support network. Don't forget to officially recognize the efforts the buddies put in helping new colleagues get settled. Make sure

---

[2]"Deadnaming is the use of the birth or other former name (i.e., a name that is "dead") of a transgender or non-binary person without the person's consent. Deadnaming may be accidental; however, it may also be used to intentionally dismiss, deny or reject a person's gender identity." *https://en.wikipedia.org/wiki/Deadnaming*

you have a way to acknowledge this type of organizational support work such as during performance evaluations or in team meetings.

Showcase Diversity

Onboarding is the ideal time to introduce new employees to your organization's DEI goals and mindset. You can explain what your organization's DEI strategy is, what types of resources and training is offered and what behavior is not tolerated in the workplace.

During these onboarding presentations, also make sure you showcase the diversity of your organization. From day one, it sets the right first impression to have visible, authentic (not token) diversity. Before inviting a speaker to present, make sure they are comfortable answering general questions on the organization's DEI goals as well.

The First 3 Months

For a new employee, onboarding does not stop after the first week. They are still in the process of learning and adjusting. This is an opportunity to continue to acknowledge your new joiners and find ways to support them and improve the onboarding experience for future new joiners.

Team Bonding

Encourage team leads to organize social events with their new joiners. You can create a catalog of suggested events and activities they can chose from and self-organize. This is a great way for new joiners to get to know their colleagues on a personal level and learn about the workplace in a casual, low-stress environment. In a remote setting, this is even harder, so if your organization is fully remote, suggest teams get together in person a few times per year.

Discrimination Reporting

Of course, you hope no employees experience discrimination or harassment in the workplace, but statistically, it will happen to some employees. Having a confusing or hidden process for reporting discrimination makes that experience even worse. Make sure your discrimination reporting process is straightforward, transparent and accessible. You can do this by including the process and contact information in the information sent to new joiners or by having a dedicated presentation on the topic. If someone is experiencing discrimination, you want to make sure the process of getting support is as easy as possible and complaints are taken seriously. This is an important step in making a safe and inclusive workplace.

Partner & Family Inclusion

When a new employee relocates with their family, the success of that transfer is also dependent on the happiness of their family members. It can be incredibly isolating to relocate with no social network in a new city. Networking and community events organized by your organization can help family members establish themselves socially. Consider offering language lessons or support in finding a new job to family members of employees who have relocated.

Feedback

Once you have implemented initiatives to increase inclusion during onboarding, you can take the opportunity to ask new employees how the experience was and how it can be improved. They now have a lot of firsthand experience with the onboarding process. This is a very valuable moment to learn from those experiences and improve on your processes. You can send out a survey or reach out directly to new joiners and ask them about their experience.

Final thoughts on onboarding

Don't think of the above initiatives like a checklist you need to replicate perfectly. It's more important to find what's right for your organization. Don't forget to recognize the progress you make towards an inclusive onboarding experience. Inclusion is an ongoing journey with no clear finish line. This can make it difficult to see the progress you have made. Try to recognize the incremental progress you make.

And finally, keep in mind the main goal: you want your employees to have a positive onboarding experience where they feel welcome and supported. And you want them to want to *stay* at your organization.[3] Inclusive onboarding is the first part of an inclusive workplace experience. It can also help employees be more productive and more engaged[4] early on. This brings you one step closer to a more inclusive and diverse organization.

Inclusive remote working

If your workplace is transitioning to a partially or fully remote working environment, take a moment to consider how inclusion fits in. In many ways, remote working unlocks many opportunities for increased inclusion, but it doesn't come automatically. There are five key inclusion practices that help employees feel included and welcome, while working remotely. All employees can utilize these practices to contribute to the inclusion of their working environment. As you are transition to remote working, communicate these practices through a blog or webinar. These tips could also be part of a bigger campaign to help employees play a role in creating an inclusive environment.

---

[3] *To Retain New Hires, Spend More Time Onboarding Them* by Ron Carucci. December 03, 2018. https://hbr.org/2018/12/to-retain-new-hires-spend-more-time-onboarding-them

[4] *How successful onboarding kickstarts employee engagement & retention* by Alex Oliver. July 31, 2020. https://www.icims.com/en-gb/blog/how-successful-onboarding-kickstarts-employee-engagement-retention/

Simulate the social interaction and trust-building

Psychological safety is necessary for creating an inclusive work environment where employees feel safe to be themselves. Building trust among colleagues creates this safety. But that trust does not come naturally. Remote working makes it more challenging to build trust and meaningful relationships. Actively create opportunities for interactions that build trust. These interactions often happen in moments when you talk with your colleagues about topics *other* than work. You can encourage this by scheduling weekly virtual coffee dates or lunches with your team. Use these as an opportunity to connect on a personal level with your colleagues to the extent to which they feel comfortable.

Engage everyone in conversations and decision making

It can be difficult to speak up and be heard in an in-person meeting, virtual meetings make this even more difficult. Because of this, it's important to intentionally create an engaging meeting format for everyone. During virtual meetings, engage all participants to get their input in the discussion. This can be as simple as noticing who is not participating and proactively asking for their input in the discussion. If one person is dominating the conversation, welcome others to contribute. Before you take a decision, make sure everyone has had a chance to give their opinion. If you are in a hybrid environment where some people are in the office and others are joining remotely, it may be better to have everyone join the meeting individually to not disadvantage the remote employees. Keep in mind the barriers that inhibit participation for everyone: language barriers, technical barriers (such as internet connection speeds) or time zone conflicts. Some meeting platforms offer live captioning, which can be helpful for colleagues with hearing issues.

Show compassion for individuals adapting to virtual working challenges

Be mindful and empathetic of everyone's home situations and arrangements. Working from home can be a challenge for those with children at home (especially single parents) or people who live in small living spaces or flat shares. For parents, be flexible with scheduling (to accommodate school schedules or child-care arrangements). Schedule meetings with 5–10 minute breaks built in to avoid meeting fatigue. Designate a few days a week as meeting-free to give people a chance to have focus time without interruptions. Normalize and accept that employees may join meetings without their cameras on.

Be thoughtful when communicating sensitive topics virtually

Delivering sensitive news or feedback virtually can add anxiety to an already stressful situation. It can also cause messages to be misunderstood or delivered harshly. This can cause a lot of uncertainty and panic, especially in a situation with low psychological safety. Make sure you are empathetic and accessible when sharing bad news and feedback. Plan to be available to discuss any open questions or follow-up actions. Offer a second call for additional questions after the employee has had a chance to process the news.

Be available and accessible

In remote work environments, it can be difficult to be visible and available to your colleagues. Employees who are earlier in their career or not as confident may not take the initiative to reach out when they need support or guidance. This can be especially relevant for employees who need help because of stigmatized issues (such as disabilities, mental health issues or other personal challenges). Be proactive to make yourself available and accessible to your team. Through intentional actions and communication, you can show that you are not burdened by them reaching out. Create a welcoming space by being open and honest and inviting your colleagues to be vulnerable without fear of consequences.

In summary, remote working presents very tangible benefits to diversity and inclusion. Employees with disabilities (non-visible and visible) may benefit from working from home by eliminating the need to commute to the office and by making their home workspace accessible to their needs. Employees with childcare or other caring responsibilities may also benefit from working from home by being nearer to the people they are caring for. Many people are simply more productive by having a home working environment and skipping the long (and sometimes expensive) commute.

Lastly, remote working typically allows organizations to hire in areas *outside of large cities* where their headquarters are located. This means you can reach a new pool of eligible applicants in different geographic regions. This is an excellent way to support equity and economic opportunity for people who live in areas without big industry sectors.

Inclusive behavior for everyone

For a workplace to truly become inclusive, employees throughout the organization (not just leaders or HR) must feel a sense of responsibility to contribute to inclusion. But employees don't always know *how* they can play an active role. They need guidance, resources and reminders to contribute. This section explores specific programs and resources that give employees the necessary tools for inclusion in the workplace.

Language

The language we use to communicate is the first area to focus on when creating an inclusive working environment. Inclusive language recognizes the importance of the words we use and the impact they have. Inclusive language is free from speech that perpetuates stereotypes, is unnecessarily gendered or discriminates.

Inclusive language prioritizes connecting empathetically with your audience and being mindful of how language and communication can impact how messages are received. It's also essential to understand the link between your organization's culture and the language used.

Communication is only one part of the culture, but the words you use are meaningful. By writing all internal communication (as well as organizational policies) in inclusive language, your organization role models the importance of inclusion top-down. Importantly, employees need support and guidance to be inclusive in their language. In an inclusive language guide, you can present the basics of inclusive language and its relevance to your organization. The appendix of this book contains an *Inclusive Language Guide.*

To make sure employees understand the concepts, offer webinars and other learning opportunities (such as a curated reading list) to invite employees to learn more and become fluent in inclusive language.

Culture Exchange Program

If your organization has employees from around the world, you already have a wealth of cultural diversity and perspectives. This is an opportunity for employees to share and learn from each other. In many ways, cultural awareness and inclusion go hand in hand. A cultural exchange is essentially a recurring event in the workplace where members of your organization voluntarily share information about their home culture and identity in a casual, friendly environment. Here's a step-by-step process to organizing a cultural exchange in the workplace, in this case, a lunchtime exchange.

1. Find a cozy space at your office with tables, chairs and sofas where people can join and bring their lunch. Alternatively, for remote working environments, schedule a recurring virtual meeting during lunch or a time that works for most of your community.

2. Create a sign-up sheet to invite people to present at the cultural exchange. Let your colleagues know the available time slots in advance and ask volunteers to add their name and culture/country next to available time slots.

3. Send out a recurring invitation to the cultural exchange that includes the link to the signup sheet. Share expectations for what to include in the cultural exchange presentation. Typically, these are casual presentations with or without slides that share interesting cultural and historical information from the employee's home country or culture.

4. Create a chat group to share announcements, materials and photos. Invite people to contribute with their own cultural additions. This could include upcoming holidays, local restaurants or where to find unique cooking ingredients.

5. Host your first exchange. Afterward, ask for feedback and use that feedback to improve the program.

Make sure not to obligate anyone to participate if they are not interested in attending or presenting. The goal here is to create a relatively low-effort ongoing program to welcome employees to share information about their culture and learn from one another. Ideally, this creates a sense of community and mutual understanding in the workplace.

Moments of inclusion

A simple program to put in place is a *Moments of Inclusion* initiative. This initiative highlights examples of small moments of inclusion through a regular blog series. It's very simple: ask employees to nominate recent behaviors or actions that have made them feel included and then celebrate these publicly in a blog series or even a poster campaign. This initiative is about role modeling inclusive behavior and inspiring others to find opportunities for small moments of inclusion in their daily work. Here are a few moments of inclusion that may be inspiring to others:

1. Proactively share your pronouns to create a welcoming space for individuals who are non-binary or transgender. Sharing pronouns shows awareness of the complexity of gender and assures everyone that you will be welcoming and consistent in using the correct pronouns of others.

2. Organize team events by asking for input from employees and trying to make an event that is fun for everyone (for example, taking care to have alcohol-free options or finding an accessible restaurant). Give everyone space to bring their interests and ideas to the table.

3. When scheduling meetings for a group, keep in mind times that would be most welcoming for parents and individuals in different time zones. Try to find a time that does not exclude your colleagues from participating.

The idea of the *Moments of Inclusion* intuitive is not to create a mandatory checklist of behaviors but to help everyone identify small moments in their life where they can bring someone else's perspective into the conversation or actively consider their needs.

Inclusive behavior for leaders

We talked about the individual responsibilities of employees to create an inclusive working environment. But what about leaders? Employees who have people management responsibility have an important role in purposefully shaping the culture of their organization. Inclusion is one part of that culture. The employees of your organization naturally see the behaviors of leaders as representative of the organization. Practically, leaders are constantly role modeling behavior whether they are doing it purposefully or not. This is the most crucial reason why you need to offer intentional skill-building and incentivizing inclusive behavior among leaders.

Practically, employees expect leaders in the organization to naturally lead the way on culture and values topics. There's a very high expectation from engaged employees for leaders (especially senior leaders and executives) to talk competently on complex DEI topics. It's possible your CEO will be invited to speak internally (or externally) on a wide range of complex topics such as intersectionality, anti-racism or trans inclusion, often on short notice. It's not wrong for employees to expect leaders to have that level of competency, but the reality is they mostly don't. Sadly, sometimes well-meaning executives are given the task to kick off a DEI event or give a short talk and they use the wrong language or make some sort of blunder. This causes a lot of frustration and pain for employees. This can also cause a breakdown of trust between the organization and its employees, which is not easily rebuilt.

But let's be clear, this skill-building takes a lot of time, energy and personal commitment (from the leaders and you in your DEI role). But the payoff is also significant. A leader who can confidently speak on these topics sets the expectations that other leaders and employees should as well. The cascading effect makes the time educating and equipping leaders very well spent.

If that's not convincing enough, a quick reminder: organizational culture is shaped by the worst behavior tolerated in your organization. Meaning, your organization can have a hundred initiatives to build inclusion in the workplace, but if the CEO makes a sexist joke and other leaders in the organization view that as appropriate workplace behavior, then the organization becomes one where sexist jokes are made and accepted. Period. Employees will *remember* that. Because of this, leaders must be mindful of their words and actions, and they must actively role model inclusive behavior. Let's explore some of the skill-building needed and the mechanisms to incentivize and amplify inclusive behavior among leaders.

Understanding DEI concepts and the WHY behind DEI

Before leaders even get into inclusion or inclusive behavior, they need to have a firm grasp of the basics. Let's first acknowledge that understanding DEI language and concepts is not easy. This is especially true for non-native English speakers who work and communicate in English. The terminology[5] can be a confusing minefield that evolves quickly. To complicate matters, there is often geographic variation in the

---

[5]DEI Glossary of terms can be helpful in building this knowledge, such as: https://ccdi.ca/media/3150/ccdi-glossary-of-terms-eng.pdf

terminology (for example, BIPOC: *Black, Indigenous, People of Color* is often preferred over POC in the US). But more than just understanding the definitions, the actual task becomes understanding the nuanced concepts and giving leaders the tools to relate to them personally and in the context of their work. Organizing a guide of terminology with a recorded webinar as well as offering drop-in sessions for leaders to ask questions in a safe space help make this tangible and accessible to them.

The next important task becomes sharing *why* inclusion is important for your particular organization. Ideally, leaders already understand this, but practically that's probably not the case. If leaders don't understand the why behind your DEI work and precisely the commitments your organization has made, they may be reluctant to put in extra effort for inclusion. Prepare a guide that explains the business impact that DEI has for your organization and the moral and social justice reasoning behind it. Include statements from your executive team in their own words that drive this home. Leaders should also be thoroughly familiar with your DEI strategy and what your priorities are. Making this content easily accessible in multiple formats, such as blogs, documents and webinar recordings, helps leaders find and access this information. Practically, leaders may need additional education through training sessions to fully grasp the *why* of your work.

Understanding inclusion and putting it into practice

Leaders need support to develop the awareness to consciously contribute to an inclusive workplace. This involves helping them understand why inclusion is necessary for the workplace and how the identity and experiences of employees impact their sense of belonging and inclusion. Leaders need to understand how privilege, marginalization and discrimination (including racism) impact inclusion in the workplace. Organizing a specific training on allyship, privilege and microaggressions will help build this understanding among leaders. This will also support building empathy and understanding of people who have different life experiences than them.

The next step is showing leaders what specific behaviors and actions are needed to be inclusive. This does not mean offering a checklist of dos and don'ts. Instead, it means helping leaders think about their personal interactions and their opportunities to role model inclusive behavior. This important to help them understand their role in an inclusive workplace.

An important part of inclusive behavior is self-awareness of one's personal actions and the impact they have on others. And another part is having the right mindset and humility to actively seek feedback and learn from it, without defensiveness. During this process, give leaders a place to discuss, request feedback or solve problems together. This exchange can happen in a private chat room or through knowledge-share sessions with their peers. Finally, don't underestimate the overall process required to educate and train leaders in inclusive behavior. This involves a series of sessions, guides and nudges that are designed to build empathy and give examples of what inclusion in the workplace practically looks like.

Creating accountability and measuring impact

Creating accountability for leaders to role model inclusive behavior is fundamental when putting this work into practice. You need to make sure this is explicitly a responsibility of leaders as well as incentivize it.

Setting the expectation that leaders should act as inclusion role models can be done by adding this into the formal expectations of the role, professional objectives or a required element in the bonus program. To be effective, this expectation needs to be communicated directly by the executive team. Executives also need to share their learning journey in understanding and putting inclusive behavior into practice. Executives can acknowledge specific inclusive behaviors of their peers and leaders within the organization in a public setting, such as on the intranet or in an All-Hands meeting. This provides tangible examples of inclusive behavior in the workplace and gives executives a chance to talk about their own learning journey.

But how can you know if these efforts are having an impact? Do employees actually feel like the organization is more inclusive than it was before? Measure this with specific questions in the inclusion and identity survey (see Part 4: *Creating an employee inclusion and identity survey*) such as "My manager demonstrates inclusive behavior." and "I am treated with dignity and respect in the workplace." When you measure the impact of these initiatives, make sure to start from a measured baseline (collected before beginning the initiatives). This allows you to see how inclusion has improved following the new initiatives.

A final note on inclusion in the workplace: Inclusion is only possible through many small actions and behaviors by everyone in your organization. It is a journey with no finish line. There is no one perfect approach that fixes all problems. Keep an eye on your progress, and you may need to test out different approaches depending on your organization's individual needs and challenges.

PART 7:
THE JOB & YOU

Many moments of success and failure have impacted my career journey. At the beginning of this book, I wrote, "DEI is not like other jobs." And as we get to the end, I'll write it again. *DEI is not like other jobs.* This work requires careful emotional distance, proactive expectation setting and constant learning and growth. While going on this journey, I took note of some of the lessons I've learned and some of the careful considerations that have helped me get in the right mindset for a meaningful career without risking burning myself out or rage-quitting.

Lessons learned

There are many common mistakes I see again and again in the DEI industry that we can all learn from, especially if you are just starting this journey. Here are the universal mistakes I've encountered.

Mistake 1: Thinking too narrowly about diversity

Obviously, diversity is not just gender, and especially not just hiring women into leadership roles. But that doesn't stop *many* organizations who are just starting their journey make this their main and only strategic focus. A solid DEI strategy should not just focus on one or two dimensions of diversity, and it should not set its goals to only empower, hire and promote women into leadership. More often than not, only white women benefit from these initiatives. A solid strategy will take a holistic approach and include race and ethnicity, sexual orientation, inclusive gender (trans and nonbinary gender), religion, disability, age diversity and more. All employees in your organization should read the strategy and feel like it is meaningful to them, no matter who they are. The rising tide lifts all boats, meaning improving the inclusion of your workplace culture will likely be felt by all employees.

When I see companies focus their DEI efforts on just creating opportunities for women, I can almost set my watch to 18 months later when they go on a difficult, reflective journey, responding to internal feedback and ultimately develop a new, more holistic strategy. Save yourself a year and a half, start with a holistic strategy from the beginning.

Mistake 2: Not recognizing your privilege and becoming defensive

When you pour a lot of your personal energy into your DEI work, it can sting to receive negative feedback or criticism. In some ways, DEI work feels thankless because you typically only receive feedback when something goes wrong or someone's expectations are not met. But feedback and criticism of your work is essential because it helps you better understand the needs of your employees and it helps you grow personally and professionally. Of course, you will not be able to satisfy everyone, but when you get feedback or criticism, listen without defensiveness, appreciate that someone cared enough to offer feedback and find a way to learn and grow from it.

Even more important, take the effort to be aware of your own privileges, no matter what they are. They surely impacted how easy or difficult it was to get hired for a DEI role, how likely your voice will be heard in a crowded room and on what topics you have lived experience. Recognizing those privileges and making space for others with less privilege plays an important role in how effective your work is. Let me speak for a moment directly to the white men and white women working in DEI. We (myself included) do not have the lived experiences of People of Color. Similarly, heterosexual people working in DEI do not have the lived experiences of people in the LGBTQI+ community. Able bodied people do know have the lived experiences of the disabled community. And of course, there's not one universal experience within those communities either, which is why it's even more important to be aware of your own privileges within the work you do. Despite working in DEI and perhaps having a lot of learned knowledge on the diversity of experiences in the world, does not automatically make anyone experts or able to speak on behalf of communities they are not a part of. There is a privilege and a responsibility in getting paid to do DEI work, while many do this work for free, *unpaid*, adding to the emotional labor in their lives. This self-awareness is critical and necessary to succeed in your work.

Mistake 3: Failure to acknowledge and address structural issues

DEI work does not exist in a vacuum. You can have a strong strategy with great initiatives. Still, if you have problematic, discriminatory or exclusionary structures in your organization undermining your efforts, it will be challenging to have impact with your work. Here's a tangible example: a diversity hiring initiative will never have long-term impact if your performance review and promotion process is discriminatory towards marginalized groups. Take the time to review processes across the board (for example: hiring, promotions, compensation, company culture, values and ethics, health care and benefits including parental leave) with an eye for equity and fairness to figure out where your problems truly lie. If you find you have systemic issues in your organization, it's best to take a pause, acknowledge those issues and address them within your strategy.

Mistake 4: Trying to accomplish too much, too fast

Everyone is optimistic when they start a new job, especially one you are passionate about. But the reality is, DEI work is painstakingly slow because it requires organizational change from the top to the bottom. When you don't accomplish your goals in the planned time, it's easy to become demotivated. Often, our stakeholders also expect very quick results with little effort. Instead, from the beginning, try to be realistic with your ambitions and plan incremental (not seismic) progress over the coming years. And importantly, give yourself the permission to reevaluate your timelines as you go.

Mistake 5: Failure to engage both executives and the grassroots

DEI work within an organization cannot be solely driven by ERGs and other employees at the grassroots level, and it cannot be driven solely top-down by leadership. The work needs to engage people throughout the organization at all levels. Having a champion from the executive team is helpful to role model behavior and embed change across the organization. Still, the ERGs and broader employee base also need to feel heard and invited to participate in the strategy implementation. Success requires a collaborative effort where all levels feel they have an active role in making change.

Mistake 6: DEI is driven only through HR

DEI as a topic is often relegated to the Human Resources department. Successful DEI work indeed requires the involvement of HR because employee processes need to be reviewed and changed. But that doesn't mean all DEI work must be driven through HR. Instead, DEI efforts should feel *embedded* in objectives and strategies throughout your organization. This specifically requires accountability from people outside of HR to truly make change. Business leaders need to feel that DEI is a responsibility for them, not just for HR.

The best model I've seen for this is having a very senior strategic DEI role sitting outside of HR, reporting directly into the executive team, supported by DEI professionals embedded across the organization including within HR. This help creates the top-down accountability while employees deployed locally are activated to get the work done.

Mistake 7: Developing a strategy or approach that is too safe

I got the feedback once: "If you aren't pissing some people off than you aren't pushing hard enough in your work." I don't always agree with this, but I think about it often. Impactful DEI work requires employees and leaders to go outside of their comfort zones, challenge their biases and assumptions and change their behavior. That process is not "comfortable" for anyone involved. You're probably going to be someone's least favorite co-worker. But that's just part of the job.

Finding the right frame of mind

This work can be emotionally draining. I've found that having the right frame of mind to be hugely important in establishing a healthy and sustainable relationship with the job. I humbly suggest a frame of mind that will help you find purpose, satisfaction and adequate emotional distance for a successful career in DEI. Let's explore some of the realities of the work.

What is a job?

This may be an obvious question, but when it comes to DEI (a topic people feel personally passionate about), it's worth being crystal clear. A job is *a financial transaction*. A transaction that exchanges your time, talent and expertise for money from the organization where you work. A job in DEI is no different. Even if you are passionate about the work and have your own personal motivations for why you do this job, it's still a job. It's not activism work in the same sense as grassroots community activism. It's a job. If you work for a for-profit company, then the leaders of your organization have their own motivation which is to make a profit. When you start to feel overwhelmed, it may be worth reminding yourself: you have no obligation to do more than what you are paid for, even if you care deeply about the topic.

Often people in DEI roles feel pressure from their organization, the employees or themselves to put their heart and soul and 110 percent of their time into the work because they are passionate about the topic. You will probably get phone calls and emails at all hours of the day and on weekends. You will also get requests to do things that are not part of your job. You will probably even get requests from friends and contacts to do DEI work for companies you don't even work at. So, to keep everything in perspective, here's an important reminder: you can be passionate about equity and justice, but that doesn't mean you need to exhaust yourself or make yourself available 24/7. Keep in mind that your stakeholders may misinterpret your passion for the job and take advantage of it. Be ready to advocate for yourself, set boundaries and say no when you need to.

Compromise means disappointing people

It's not realistic or possible for all your stakeholders to get exactly what they want all the time. A lot of DEI work centers on getting two people who have very different motivations to compromise. It's great if you can find solutions where everyone gets what they want. But more likely, success means finding a compromise that roughly works for everyone involved but likely somewhat disappoints both sides. As the mediator of these compromises, it doesn't always feel like a success, even when you've reached an agreement. But it's the reality of the work and making everyone happy is truly an impossible goal.

Find your own way to judge your success

DEI is particularly hard because it can be difficult to know when you are succeeding or whether the impact of your work is felt. We covered this in the section on Part 3: *How to measure the impact of your work*. But beyond that, how should you interpret or weigh the feedback you receive from different stakeholders? Here's one way to think about it: ask yourself, whose lives are you trying to benefit, who would you like to feel the impact of your work? Michelle MiJung Kim of Awaken sums it up well in this tweet[1] "In case you need to hear this today: Don't measure the success of your D&I work by the praises of cis white men. Measure the success of the program by the sigh of relief and validation from queer and trans black women." At the end of the day, if the white, male CEO thinks you are doing a great job, but the members of your ERGs don't feel the impact, it's a good time to take a pause and re-evaluate whether your work is having the right impact for the employees in your organization.

You can't be successful as the lone voice of DEI

Now, here is the tough love part. In my personal opinion, it's not reasonable or sustainable to act as the sole voice of inclusion and equity in your organization. If you are the sole person working in DEI *and* your organization is not willing to back you up and support your work, it's probably not worth your time and energy. Try your best to figure out whether your organization is acting with you *or against you*. Are they willing to put the time, resources and prioritization behind your work or

---

[1] Michelle MiJung Kim (@mjmichellekim) on Twitter, May 30, 2019: https://twitter.com/mjmichellekim/status/1133969227398897666

are they constantly fighting against you and throwing you under the bus? You will probably be able to figure this out quickly as you try to implement initiatives and naturally face barriers. It's how the organization supports you in breaking down those barriers that matters.

And separately, try to understand how the organization perceives your role. Do they see you as an expert and a leader that drives change or a fixer who cleans up messes? Or even worse, do they see you as a figurehead who ticks a box? Sometimes these are painful questions to investigate. But your time is valuable; your energy and insight are valuable. You could be doing ANYTHING with your time and energy, but you chose this organization and this role. If your work is not appreciated and you are constantly banging your head against the wall, find something else.

Protecting yourself from burnout

You cannot pour from an empty cup. You must take care of yourself in order to find satisfaction and happiness in all parts of your life, including your professional work. If you do not have the strength and patience for empathy, it's hard to do such an emotionally intense job. Here are some considerations to help you protect yourself from burnout and emotional fatigue.

Set emotional boundaries

This work is intensely emotional and much more draining than most typical 9-to-5 jobs. It's important to acknowledge the emotional effort it takes. Take time for self-care and to recharge. Say no to extra work, find and respect your own boundaries. Be thoughtful about how you spend your free time in order to recharge and preserve your energy. Make sure you take time off throughout the year, especially when you need a rest or feel close to burning out. *Never leave vacation days unused.* And just in case it needs to be said: when you are sick, take a sick day! The job can wait - remember it's just a job!

Find your support network

It can be very therapeutic to commiserate with others who are tackling similar challenges. Try to find a group of friends or colleagues who can empathize with the frustrations of the work and can act as sparring partners to problem-solve or simply offer perspective and support.

Know when to quit and move on

A few years ago, I was on a panel, and someone in the audience asked: "What would you do if the CEO in your organization was accused of sexual harassment? As a DEI leader, how would you personally handle this?" Another panelist replied: "I would see whether the organization is legitimately interested in taking action or whether they'd just try to sweep it under the rug. If it were the latter, I'd absolutely leave." I think about this often. I've found it important to identify the intersection of my personal values and the job I am doing. Ask yourself: have there been critical moments in your career when you feel like there is a true conflict between your values and the organization where you work? If an organization is asking you to significantly compromise your values and integrity in order to do the work, then there is not a match between you and the job (and they probably don't perceive you as a leader, but as a fixer). You do not have any obligation to fix a system that is beyond broken, especially if no one in leadership is seriously willing to provide the tools to fix it.

To sum it all up: keep your work in perspective. You do not have to play a superhero, saving an organization from its worst behavior. You do not have to work yourself to exhaustion or burnout because you are passionate about the work you do. You are doing the work you are paid to do. And you could be doing absolutely anything, so make sure the work is worth your time.

CLOSING THOUGHTS

Writing this book has been in itself a personal journey. A lot of the words in these chapters were already written in some form, either as a blog post or ideas scrawled in notebooks. Putting it together as a logical, self-contained narrative presented a good opportunity for me to reflect. As I finished writing, I had many conversations with friends and colleagues about the main themes and learnings they recognize in their career paths. I thought I'd share some of these below to again reiterate that we are often struggling with the same challenges, and there is comfort and solidarity in numbers.

Dealing with the emotional weight of the work and being present

Oftentimes, we as DEI professionals get looped in after a business decision was made and we are asked to advise on how to remediate the DEI risk generated by that decision. In many ways, it's the nature of the job. We have the power and influence to make the best of a difficult situation. But on the other hand, even if these situations do not have an impact on us personally, there still may be harmful or hurtful to our colleagues. Dealing with the fallout of business decisions and how it personally affects our colleagues can be more difficult to weather.

One colleague recently shared with me that they try not to take anything personally in their daily DEI work. They focus on maintaining resilience in order to be available for their coworkers. They reminded me "We're not doing this only for ourselves, we're doing this for a community of people. We are trying to change a workplace, an institution. This requires me to be present 100%. I can't afford to be distracted."

Activism or education?

Activism and the desire to see change in the world may be one of the motivations for the work we do. And up unto a point, it works in the workplace. But we also need to translate the activist's message into language and actions that organizations understand. We need to meet our stakeholders where they are, with patience. And even though it can be painful to repeatedly explain the why of DEI or answer poorly informed questions, it's also the crux of our work. On this topic, Aubrey Blanche writes: "It's a *lot* of answering very basic questions with a smile. In my personal time, I don't have to answer basic questions about meritocracy. In my job, I have opted in to answering these questions. Repeatedly. With compassion. 4000 times."[1]

---

[1] *How can I get a job in DEI (Part 1)?* Aubrey Blanche, 2019. https://blog.usejournal.com/how-can-i-get-a-d-i-job-bcc0b32a3c81

I sometimes remind myself that even if some parts of the work are disappointing and demoralizing, it's all part of the job. We can't create change without helping people go on their own learning journey and personally feel the value of DEI. In many ways, it's a prerequisite to the next phase… activating our stakeholders to drive DEI within *their* work, which is critical to our success.

Advocacy and allyship without causing harm

For our stakeholders in the workplace who are passionate but privileged advocates, contributing in some way to DEI efforts is a natural place for them to channel their desire to be a part of the collective fight for equity and justice. But sadly, in these situations, I've seen how easily their voices and calls for action drown out the needs of individuals who are part of marginalized groups. Advising these passionate, *well-meaning* allies on when to be silent to let others speak becomes another important task of our role.

An outlook on the future

Reflecting also prompted me to think about how all the individual projects, goals and ambitions of this job fit together like puzzle pieces to form a broader career. Through that, I thought about DEI as a *profession* and where the industry might be headed.

What does the future of DEI in the workplace hold? Despite more senior roles being created in DEI with titles of Director, VP and CDO, still many companies in Europe struggle to approach DEI with the proper resourcing and commitment needed to be effective. I'm often disappointed to see the sole person working on DEI in a 2,000+ person company having the title of *Jr. HR Manager*, *Intern* or *Working Student*. I'm even more disheartened when I talk with them and hear how they struggle in their role. I see it as a reflection of just how much (or how little) an organization cares about DEI.

However, bits of progress in the past few years have been encouraging. I've seen many newly created DEI positions report directly into their executive team. I've seen job postings that emphasize that the Director of DEI will lead a team instead of managing as a lone practitioner. I've seen budgets of DEI teams and salaries of DEI practitioners increase across the board. I've seen more organizations publish a DEI strategy with measurable commitments (some ambitious, some less so). And importantly, I've seen organizations in Europe finally willing to collect data on how diverse and inclusive they are. This is a critical step to be able to measure future progress. This gives me hope.

Sadly, I've also seen the rise of new organizations that sell rankings and awards for companies to tout their success against their competitors. This gives me less hope. I wish these added value and resources to the DEI ecosystem, but to me, they seem more like pay-to-rank schemes for branding and PR. Most seem to lack awareness about actual ambitious DEI goals and are missing substance for tracking and follow-through.

I'm interested to see what the future holds, especially as an economic down-turn may be in front of us. Will DEI continue to be the hot topic it has been for the past two years? Or will it be the first to be cut? Let's see.

Final thoughts

Writing this book has helped me consider and process my own conflicted feelings I have about working in DEI. I have had moments of great pride and moments of great disappointment. For some of my stakeholders I will always be moving too slowly, for others I will always be pushing too hard. This combination of disappointment and frustration can take a toll. But through this, there has always been learning and growth.

I hope this book has also given you some perspective and helpful tools to think about the work we do and how to do it better. The reflection questions in the appendix are particularly crafted to help you think about how each chapter is relevant to your work and how you can put the guidance into practice.

Surely, I didn't have every answer you were looking for, but I hope this book could somehow help you. And perhaps, it can be a jumping-off point for some productive and fulfilling work ahead or simply a gentle reminder to take some time off for self-care and rest!

APPENDIX

Inclusion & Identity Survey Questions

This section includes example questions which could be used in an Inclusion and Identity survey. Not all of these will be relevant for your organization, you will need to adapt the questions to be appropriate for your community and relevant to your geographic location.

Example Inclusion Survey Questions

The inclusion questions are based on a Likert scale with the following options:

    a. Strongly agree
    b. Agree
    c. Neither agree nor disagree
    d. Disagree
    e. Strongly disagree

These questions have been sourced from draft inclusion survey questions available online.

Belonging & Authenticity

1. I can be myself at work.
2. While at work, I am comfortable expressing opinions that are different from my team.
3. My opinion is valued.
4. In my team, people's ideas are judged on their quality, not on the personal characteristics of those who express them.
5. I plan to be working at [Organization] two years from now.

Equity and Respectful Treatment

1. The people I work with are respectful to one another.

2. At [Organization], I am treated with respect.
3. Administrative tasks that don't have a specific owner (e.g., taking notes in meetings, scheduling events, cleaning up shared spaces) are fairly divided at [Organization].

Inclusive Behavior

1. My manager demonstrates inclusive behavior.
2. Senior leadership are prepared to manage a diverse workforce.
3. I am included in any business decisions that impact my work.

Opportunity to Succeed

1. Everyone at [Organization] has a fair opportunity to succeed.
2. I have fair access to opportunities, projects and training that would allow me to grow professionally.
3. My job challenges me to learn and grow my skills.
4. Promotion decisions are fair at [Organization].
5. My job performance is evaluated fairly.
6. I believe that my total compensation is fair, relative to similar roles at [Organization].

Safety & Needs

1. [Organization] demonstrates a strong commitment to meeting the needs of employees with disabilities.
2. I know how to report instances of harassment or discrimination
3. I believe [Organization] would take appropriate action if an instance of harassment or discrimination was reported.

Example Identity Survey Questions

1. Which race and ethnicity group or groups do you identify with? (multiselect)

With the intention for the survey to be globally relevant, the following list represents broad identity groups which may not be adequate for your own self identification. Select the group or groups you identify with most. You may self describe in addition to, or instead of, selecting from the list.

a. Asian:
    i.   East Asian
    ii.   South Asian
    iii. Southeast Asian
    iv. Central Asian
    v.   Other

b. Black:
    i.   African Heritage
    ii.   Caribbean Heritage
    iii. Afro-Latinx Heritage
    iv. Other

c. White
d. Indigenous (including Aboriginal, Native American and First Nations)
e. Latinx, Latin American or Hispanic
f. North African and West Asian also known as Middle Eastern
g. Pacific Islander (including Micronesia, Melanesia, and Polynesia)
h. Traveller or Roma
i. Self describe
j. I would rather not say

2. Does the race and ethnicity group or groups you selected above match the majority group of where you live?
a. Yes
b. No
c. I would rather not say

3. Which of the following best describes your gender?
[Organization] fully recognizes self-determination of all gender identities and support people in living as their authentic selves.
a. Woman
b. Man
c. Gender Queer or Non-binary
d. Self describe

e. I would rather not say

4. Are you transgender?

Transgender is an umbrella term which refers to any person whose gender identity and/or gender expression differs from the sex assigned to them at birth.

a. Yes
b. No
c. I would rather not say

5. Which of the following best describes your sexual orientation?

a. Gay or Lesbian
b. Heterosexual / Straight
c. Bisexual
d. Pansexual
e. Asexual
f. Queer
g. Self describe
h. I would rather not say

6. What is your age?

a. 16-24 years old
b. 25-34 years old
c. 35-44 years old
d. 45-54 years old
e. 55-64 years old
f. 65 years and older
g. I would rather not say

7. Do you have a visible or non-visible disability? (multiselect)

Disability refers to any condition, either physical or mental, not limited to any legal definition of disability, that impacts one or more life activities.

a. Yes, visible disability
b. Yes, non-visible disability
c. No

    d.   I would rather not say

8. Do you consider yourself neurodiverse?

    a.   Yes

    b.   No

    c.   I would rather not say

9. What is your Religion? (multiselect)

    a.   Muslim

    b.   Bahai

    c.   Christian

    d.   Catholic

    e.   Buddhist

    f.   Jewish

    g.   Hindu

    h.   Agnostic

    i.   Atheist

    j.   Non-religiously spiritual

    k.   Self describe

    l.   I would rather not say

10. Does you or your family have a migration or refugee background? (multiselect)

    a.   Yes, I do

    b.   Yes, my parents or grandparents do

    c.   No

    d.   I would rather not say

11. Do you have anyone who depends on you for care? (multiselect)

    a.   Yes, a child or children

    b.   Yes, an adult family member

    c.   No

    d.   I would rather not say

12. What is the highest degree or education level that you have achieved?
    a. Less than high school, secondary school or equivalent
    b. Upper secondary, high school or equivalent
    c. Apprenticeship, Trade Qualification or Associate Degree
    d. Bachelor's Degree or equivalent
    e. Master's Degree or equivalent
    f. Doctorate or Advanced Degree
    g. I would rather not say

13. Do you consider yourself a first-generation college graduate?
    Being a first-generation college graduate means that you are the first person in your immediate family to attend college or university.
    a. Yes
    b. No
    c. I would rather not say

14. Is the language you use most often at work your first language?
    a. Yes
    b. No
    c. I would rather not say

15. What is your Nationality?
    Select from a list of Nationalities
    a. I would rather not say

16. How long have you worked at [Company]?
    a. Less than 6 months
    b. 6-12 months
    c. 1-2 years
    d. 2-4 years
    e. 4-6 years
    f. 6-10 years
    g. More than 10 years
    h. I would rather not say

Job Ad Diversity Statement

This example job ad diversity statement can be adapted for your needs. If you have a publicly available website or blogpost that explains your commitment to DEI or DEI strategy, link it within the statement.

"We don't look for culture fit, but culture-add. We value all the perspectives our team members bring to the table, and we encourage YOU to apply, even if you do not fit 100 percent of the requirements. We welcome everyone to apply, especially those who are underrepresented in the industry, including but not limited to People of Color, LGBTQI+ folks, women, individuals with disabilities (both visible and non-visible), and people of any age or family status.

We understand the value that diversity brings to our organization, and we strive to create a working environment that is inclusive, psychologically and physically safe and ensures everyone can be heard and their contributions valued. We know that diversity makes us stronger and more successful, and we also know it takes an inclusive workplace with a strong sense of belonging to fully empower everyone. We are committed to making a consistent, top-down effort to role model a strong understanding of diversity, inclusion and belonging and demonstrate inclusive behaviors in the workplace. We take conscious efforts to prevent discrimination on the basis of race, color, ancestry, religion, national origin, sexual orientation, age, citizenship, marital or family status, political views, disability, gender identity or expression or any other identity."

Inclusive Language Guide

What is inclusive Language?

Inclusive language refers to communicating in a way that expresses respect and openness towards individuals and groups while avoiding terms or assumptions that hurt or exclude people. Inclusive language makes sure your audience feels welcome and helps them better relate to your message.

Language is constantly evolving. Because of this, inclusive terms we use also change. Specifically, terms referring to identity and communities tend to change frequently. Why is that? DEI Communications expert Samet Akti shares: "Names for marginalized groups continue to change as long as people have negative attitudes towards them. This is how language works. Descriptors will be in flux as long as our relationships will be, too."[1]

Why is inclusive language important?

Language influences human thinking and plays a role in shaping behavior and perceptions. Inclusive language helps reduce bias that is coded into the language we use. Using inclusive language demonstrates a conscious effort to communicate in a way that demonstrates respect, acceptance and inclusion. To understand why inclusive language is important, *think about what you are ultimately trying to achieve:* You want to build trustworthy and meaningful relationships with your colleagues, partners or customers, where everyone feels welcome. Inclusive communication helps build these relationships.

---

[1] "What is the Euphemism Treadmill?" LinkedIn post by Samet Akti
https://www.linkedin.com/posts/sametakti_3-di-nuance-euphemism-treadmill-activity-6924981079443402753-Af_A/

Core principles of inclusive language

1) Non-discriminatory language

Avoid language that is discriminatory or hurtful to an individual or group of people, based on their identity. Avoid adding labels or descriptions to groups of people unless it is directly relevant to the content. For example, in a press release about fundraising of a new technology startup, it's not necessary to mention personal identity details about the founders unless it's relevant to the topic.

2) Stereotypes and assumptions

Through language, prejudices can be reinforced. Consider counter-stereotypical examples and avoid defaulting to common stereotypes or scenarios that you see regularly. Be careful to avoid statements that play into stereotypes about groups of people. Consider whether you're reinforcing a stereotype, even if the description is viewed as positive. Stereotypes of a particular group of people can be harmful and limiting, even when intended as a compliment. For example, referring to people with disabilities as courageous, brave or superhuman for simply living their lives is condescending and insinuates that it's exceptional for someone with a disability to be successful.

3) Gender-sensitive language

Gender-sensitive language means being inclusive of all gender identities (including identities beyond binary gender); not making assumptions about a person's gender and avoiding language that perpetuates gender stereotypes. To do this, use gender neutral terms when you are referring to people of all genders, rather than the generic masculine version (e.g., Chairman → Chair or Chairperson). Be mindful to not use language that makes assumptions that people conform to a gender binary (e.g., Welcome ladies & gentlemen → Welcome everyone). Share your pronouns proactively and consistently use the correct pronouns for people you are speaking about. If you make a mistake, correct yourself, learn from the mistake and move on.

4) Representation

Take care to notice when groups of people are systematically not mentioned or they are made to feel unimportant. When creating content, take a moment to consider who is represented and who may be left out. If you are referring to families, include examples of same-sex partners and a range of family structures. Consider various communication approaches to find the best way to communicate with your audience (such as videos, blogs, visuals or podcasts) so your message resonates with people who like to consume messaging in different formats. This can be particularly inclusive of people who are neurodiverse or are non-native speakers of the language you are communicating in.

5) Cultural & Geographic Awareness

Be aware of culturally significant dates, customs and language. This awareness help to show respect to your audience. Cultural norms vary so make an effort to communicate in a culturally sensitive way which could include using a title (Mrs., Ms., Mx., Mr.) or adjusting the formality of your tone. When talking about holidays or celebrations, include a range of holidays, and don't assume everyone celebrates the holidays you are familiar with. Be mindful of geographic differences, for example seasons (Spring, Summer, Autumn, Winter) occur at different times of the year geographically or world events that impact your audience.

6) Respect for the language people use to describe themselves

Language is constantly evolving, and individuals will have preferences as to the language they prefer for themselves, which may change over time. 'Nothing about us, without us' is a good rule to follow - if you're talking about or to a specific group or community, make sure you get input from members of that group. Within a specific community, there may be differing opinions and stances on a preferred language and this may mean using different language for different people. If you're speaking about or to a specific person, sensitively ask which terms they prefer.

Do you want to learn more about inclusive language? I can recommend working with Fair Language: *https://www.fairlanguage.com/*

Reflection Questions

These questions will help you apply the guidance in each chapter to the work you are doing in your organization.

PART 1: INTRODUCING ORGANIZATIONAL DEI

1. How is your organization set up? Are there hierarchy levels? Are there business units or locations with different DEI needs?
2. Is the scope of your DEI role internal with a focus on employees or does it also include external DEI with a focus on customers?
3. Who are the key stakeholders you will need to support you?
4. Do you already have working relationships with those stakeholders?

PART 2: UNDERSTANDING WHAT IT TAKES

1. Are senior leaders willing to contribute their visibility and support to your organization's DEI work?
2. Do you have a budget to support your organization's DEI work?
3. Are stakeholders across your organization willing to contribute time and resources for DEI initiatives?
4. Are there skills you'd like to build to support you in your work?
5. Do you need the expertise and services of external consultants to get started?

PART 3: SETTING UP FOR SUCCESS

1. In your executive team, who champions DEI work in your organization?
2. Is your DEI council diverse and representative of your entire organization?
3. Does your strategy holistically address diversity, equity and inclusion, without prioritizing or focusing on only one or two identities?
4. Has your executive team committed to the strategy and provided the resources needed to put it into practice?
5. What measurable KPIs will help you understand the impact of your work?

PART 4: EVERYTHING ABOUT EMPLOYEE RESOURCE GROUPS

1. Do employees who would like to start a new ERG understand the necessary steps and what support is available to them?
2. Do stakeholders and leaders in your organization understand the value of ERGs and how to collaborate with them?
3. Do ERG organizers feel recognized and rewarded for their contributions to their ERG?
4. Are ERG leaders more or less likely to stay longer with your organization than employees not involved in ERGs?

PART 5: DEEP DIVE: IMPACTFUL DEI INITIATIVES

1. How would an inclusion and identity survey help you better understand the DEI challenges of your organization?
2. Is there ownership and accountability of DEI throughout your organization?
3. Which diversity hiring initiatives have been most successful for your organization? Which initiatives have been least successful?
4. Is your organization a welcoming place for new hires who are underrepresented in your organization or industry?
5. How could a partnership with an external organization help you achieve your DEI goals?

PART 6: DEEP DIVE: CREATING INCLUSION IN THE WORKPLACE

1. Are new employees offered a welcoming and inclusive onboarding experience?
2. Is your remote working policy inclusive and flexible to suit the needs of all employees?
3. Do employees have opportunities to learn about inclusion and how they can contribute to an inclusive workplace?
4. Do leaders in your organization have opportunities to grow their skills to become more inclusive leaders?

PART 7: THE JOB & YOU

1. Do you have a good understanding of what is inside and outside your sphere of impact and control?

2. Are you able to recognize when you feel overwhelmed or exhausted on the job?

3. Are you comfortable managing expectations and setting boundaries with your colleagues?

4. Are you comfortable saying no to requests or ideas that you do not have the capacity to implement?

5. Do you have a support network you can reach out to in order to process the emotional toll of the job?

Further Reading

PART 1: INTRODUCING ORGANIZATIONAL DEI

Inclusion: Diversity, the New Workplace & the Will to Change by Jennifer Brown

Inclusive 360: Proven Solutions for an Equitable Organization by Bernadette Smith

PART 2: UNDERSTANDING WHAT IT TAKES

Demanding More: Why Diversity and Inclusion Don't Happen and What You Can Do About It by Sheree Atcheson

INdivisible: Radically Rethinking Inclusion for Sustainable Business Results by Alison Maitland and Rebekah Steele

The Wake Up: Closing the Gap Between Good Intentions and Real Change by Michelle MiJung Kim

PART 3: SETTING UP FOR SUCCESS

The Financial Times Guide to Inclusion and Diversity: Your Comprehensive Guide to Implementing a Successful I&D Strategy by Vikki Leach

The Loudest Duck: Moving Beyond Diversity while Embracing Differences to Achieve Success at Work by Laura A. Liswood

PART 4: EVERYTHING ABOUT EMPLOYEE RESOURCE GROUPS

The ERG Handbook: Everything You Wanted to Know about Employee Resource Groups but Didn't Know Who to Ask by Aimee K. Broadhurst

Employee Resource Group Excellence: Grow High Performing ERGs to Enhance Diversity, Equality, Belonging, and Business Impact by Robert Rodriguez

Printed in Great Britain
by Amazon